# CHEMISTRY

# Science of
# PALMISTRY

By
**Edward Heron-Allen**

**PILGRIMS PUBLISHING**
◆ Varanasi ◆

**SCIENCE OF PALMISTRY**
EDWARD HERON-ALLEN

*Published by:*
PILGRIMS PUBLISHING

*An imprint of:*
**PILGRIMS BOOK HOUSE**
*(Distributors in India)*
B 27/98 A-8, Nawabganj Road
Durga Kund, Varanasi-221010, India
Tel: 91-542- 2314060,
Fax: 91-542- 2312456
E-mail: pilgrims@satyam.net.in
Website: www.pilgrimsbooks.com

*Edited by Christopher N Burchett*
*Cover design by Sasya*
*Layout by Asha*

ISBN: 81-7769-045-0

*Printed in India at Pilgrim Press Pvt. Ltd. Lalpur Varanasi*

# Contents

# INTRODUCTION TO THE NEW EDITION

Cheiromancy or Palmistry, as it is more popularly known these days, is an ancient art cum science, which has bemused people throughout the ages. Although not considered an exact science by the majority of Astrologers it is still by far the most popular form of predicting the future. The common man on the street is always willing to have his hand read by anyone he presumes is capable of doing so.

Heron-Allen has brought us down to earth in his detailed description of Palmistry or Cheiromancy as he likes to refer to it. He makes it quite clear throughout his very detailed and explicit book that Palmistry is not for the charlatans to befool the public at large but rather a serious and very exacting subject which requires much more than a cursory knowledge to predict a persons future. So beware of the persons who have little or no knowledge of this exacting subject for if you really wish to have your hand read, go to a person who is known to have studied and perfected this art.

Not unlike Astrology, Palmistry has always played a great role in moulding people's lives. There was a time in history when no King or Emperor worth his salt did not employ persons gifted with the powers of reading ones palms. How many decisions of the greatest importance were made only after consultations with oracles or astrologers? Even in more recent times examples of heads of state can be found who always confer with astrologers or palmists before making decisions of great importance.

The author has very lucidly and succinctly explained much of the reasoning behind the making of predictions after observation of subjects' hands. It becomes clear whilst reading this book that there is a lot more to palm reading than meets the eye.

Christopher N Burchett
June 2001
VARANASI

# FOREWORD

Cheiromancy is that branch of the science of cheirosophy which reveals not only the habits and temperaments of men, but also the events of their past, the conditions of their present, and the circumstances of their future lives, by the inspection and interpretation of the formations of the palm of the hand, and the lines which are traced thereon. It is necessary that in making a cheirognomic examination of a subject the inspection should be conducted with a due regard to the cheiromancy of the hands; it will be seen immediately how much more important it is that the shapes of the hands and fingers should be considered in giving a cheiromantic explanation of any submitted palm. For what is clearer and more easily to be understood than that the character and temperament of a man (chiefly revealed by the cheirognomic examination, of his hands) should very greatly influence, even if it does not absolutely bring about, the events which are recorded in his palms, so that, a glance at the fingers and thumb will nearly always explain anything which appears doubtful in the palm, and by making a preliminary cheirognomic exami-nation of a subject, the cheiromantic examination will be rendered very much clearer and easier of interpretation. Therefore, as we shall immediately see, I shall combine cheirognomy with cheiro-mancy far more than I combine cheiromancy with cheirognomy, [because we had not yet entered upon the consideration of this more complicated branch,] with a view to rendering my exposition easier of remembrance.

## Mounts of the palm

We shall consider in turn, the mounts and the lines of the palm, with the signs and other modifications which it is necessary to bear in mind; but first, we must arrive at a complete understanding of the various parts of the hand, of the lines traced in the palm, and of the names by which they are known to cheirosophists.

And I take this opportunity of pointing out that the names given to the Mounts [those of the principal planets] are not given to them by reason of any astrological signification which they were at one time supposed to bear, but because we have been accustomed to connect certain characte-ristics with certain gods of the pagan mythology, and because it is therefore convenient to give to the formations of the hand which reveal certain characteristics, the names of the particular gods whose characteristics those were; a principle obviously more reasonable than to describe geographically in every instance the locality [in the hand] of the formation which it is desired to designate; a course which would inevitably culminate in a confusion only to be expected from the continual reiteration of an indicative verbosity. I shall therefore be understood not to be using the expressions in the old astrologic sense when I make use of such terms as "The Mount of Venus," or "The Plain of Mars," but merely to be indicating the characteristic betrayed by a development of the hand at a certain point.

# CHAPTER ONE

## LINES OF THE PALM

### The Map of the Hand

On Plate I, you will find a complete map of the hand, whereon is written the specific and technical name given to each part thereof, the mounts being indicated in their proper position by the planetary signs for the sake of brevity and clearness.

The thumb is consecrated to Venus, and at its base will be found the Mount of Venus, surrounded by the line of life. The base, or "ball" of the thumb, is frequently looked upon as a phalanx distinct from the hand, but, cheirosophically speaking, the thumb has but two phalanges, this base being termed the Mount of Venus.

The first finger [or index] is that of Jupiter, and at its base [i.e., immediately below it, at the top of the palm] will be found the Mount of Jupiter.

The second finger [or middle finger] is that of Saturn, and the mount which should be found immediately below it is the Mount of Saturn.

The third finger [or ring finger] is termed the finger of Apollo [or of the Sun], and the Mount of Apollo will be found, if present, at its base.

The fourth finger [or little finger] is that of Mercury, whose mount will in like manner be found immediately beneath it.

Just below the Mount of Mercury [between the line of heart and the line of head] is the Mount of Mars.

Underneath this last mount and extending from it to the wrist, is found the Mount of the Moon.

The whole of the centre of the palm is occupied by the plain or Triangle of Mars, which is comprised between the line of life, the line of head, and the Mounts of Mars and of the Moon.

## The Triangle

This part of the hand is also called the triangle, and is composed of the upper

2

angle—i.e., that formed by the junction of the lines of life and of head; the inner angle——i.e., that formed by the junction of the line of head with the line of health or the line of fate, at the Mount of the Moon; and the lower angle, which is formed by the appro-ximation or junction of the line of life and the line of health [when the latter is present].

The quadrangle is the rectangular space comprised between the lines of head and of heart, and is generally bounded on the one side by the line of fate and on the other by the line of Apollo.

The rascette or restreinte is the point on the wrist at which it joins the hand, which is generally occupied by one or more lines, which are more or less apparent, the upper one of which is known as the rascette and the others as the restreintes, the whole forming what are called the Bracelets of Life.

The lines generally found in the hands are as follows:— The line of life, which encircles the ball of the thumb or Mount of Venus:

The line of head, which, starting form the beginning of the line of life [to which

# Plate I

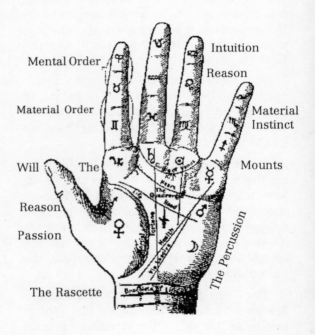

Mental Order

Intuition

Reason

Material Order

Material Instinct

Will    The

Mounts

Reason

Passion

The Percussion

The Rascette

## The Map of the Hand

it is usually joined], between the thumb and first finger, runs straight across the hand:

The line of heart, which, starting from the Mounts of Jupiter or of Saturn, runs across the hand immediately below the Mounts of Saturn, Apollo, and Mercury, ending at the percussion:

The line of fate or fortune, which, starting either from the line of life, from the rascette, or from the Mount of the Moon, runs up more or less directly to the middle finger [the finger of Saturn]:

The line of health or liver, which, starting near the wrist, at the base of the line of life, rises diagonally across the hand to meet the line of head, close to the Mount of Mars, or at the top of the mount of the moon: *and*

The line of art and brilliancy, which, rising from the triangle or its vicinity rises to the finger of Apollo [the third], cutting across the mount at its base.

To these are added three lesser lines sometimes found in a hand, which are:— The line of Mars, which lies close inside the line of life, which it follows as a sister line.

The ring or girdle of Venus, which encloses the Mounts of Saturn and of Apollo; *and*

The Via Lasciva, or milky way, which, rising from the wrist, traverses the Mount of the Moon.

The principal lines are also known by other technical names, which [to avoid repetition] will sometimes be used in the following pages. Thus the line of life is also called the Vital. The line of head is also called the Natural. The line of heart is also called the Mensal. The line of fortune is also called the Saturnian. The line of art or brilliancy is also called the Apollonian, and the line of health is often known as the Hepatic.

## Twelve phalanges of the fingers

The ancient Cheiromants used also to consider the twelve phalanges of the fingers, as representing the twelve signs of the Zodiac, and used therefrom to predict the seasons at which certain events would come to pass. This is a branch of cheirosophy which, it is needless to say, is now obsolete, having been refined away with the rest of the dross which used to disguise the pure metal of the science; but Miss Horsley has put them into the diagram at my request, as they may be interesting to my readers.

Having, therefore, mastered what may be called the geography of the hand, we can now turn to the consideration of the cheiromancy of the hand, commencing, as I have said, with the mounts, and continuing with the lines; but before entering into the minute discussion and examination of each particular mount and of each particular line, I wish to devote a sub-section to the enunciation of certain general principles, which, applying to all mounts and lines equally, must be carefully borne in mind throughout every cheiromantic examination.

Note. – It has been suggested to me that I should have opened this work with a sub-section, devoted to an explanation of the modus operandi of cheirosophy, of the method in which the cheirosophist should proceed when he undertakes the cheirosophic examination of a subject; but I have reflected that it is of no use deferring the real business of the book by teaching my readers how to put into

# Plate II

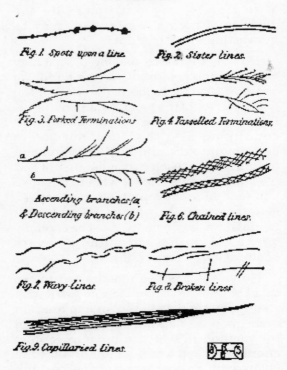

Fig. 1. Spots upon a line.

Fig. 2. Sister lines.

Fig. 3. Forked Terminations.

Fig. 4. Tasselled Terminations.

Ascending branches (a)
& Descending branches (b)

Fig. 6. Chained lines.

Fig. 7. Wavy Lines.

Fig. 8. Broken Lines.

Fig. 9. Capillaried Lines.

## Conditions of the Lines

practice principles which they have not yet acquired – a thing paradoxical in itself. I have, therefore, relegated this matter to the conclusion of the work, as being the more appropriate position for such a sub-section.

## Lines and Disposition

Livid lines, with a tendency towards blackish-ness, betray a melancholy and often a revengeful disposition. Such subjects are grave in demeanour and cunning in character, affable, but haughty; and these indications are the more certain if the fingers are long and the thumb is broad.

Black spots upon a line indicate always nervous diseases, whilst livid holes betray the presence of an organic affection of the part corresponding with the line [Fig. I, Plate II.]. It must be noted that, however well coloured lines may be, a feeble development of the mounts will counteract their good indications.

The ancient cheiromants used to affirm that people who had been born in the daytime had the lines clearer marked in the them more apparent in the left; a statement which we must class with the dicta laid down for ascertaining birthdays noted in another place; they also stated that the former resembled their fathers, whilst the latter took after their mothers.

It must also be noted that lines may enlarge, diminish, and even disappear, so that the province of the cheirosophist is, as I have said below, to indicate the present condition and indications of the lines, and the likelihood of their future modification. There is one thing to be noted in connection with this matter, which is, that the indications of cunning never alter or become modified; cunning being a characteristic which is acquired, and a characteristic thus acquired is never lost by a weak character on account of inability to free itself, nor by a strong one from a disinclination to do so.

Again, in reading the lines a single indication must never be accepted as final, especially if it is a bad one. To make any indication certain [whether good or bad] corroborating signs must be sought for in both hands, and the absence of corroboration in one hand will contradict, or at any rate greatly modify, any evil sign in the other. A single sign only affords a presumption of the tendency or event which it indicates, and the cause of the danger must be found in the aspect of the mounts, and other lines of the palm, or the development and formations of the whole hand. In the same way the indication of prudence in the second joint of the thumb will go far towards modifying an evil prediction, which may be found in the palm.

## Sister lines

When any principal line is accompanied throughout its course by a second line lying close to it, the principal line is greatly strengthened and benefited by this "sister line." as it is called. The consecutiveness of the sister will contradict the evils foreshadowed by a break in the principal line, but if both are broken, the evils are the more certainly to be feared [fig. 2. Plate II.].

If the hand is covered with a multiplicity, a network of little lines which cross one another in all directions, it betrays a mental agitation and dissatisfaction with one's surroundings and oneself. It is always the outcome of a highly nervous temperament; and in a soft spatulate hand these little lines denote hypochondria.

A fork at the end of a line is often a good, for it increases the powers of the lines without carrying them too far. At the same time it often indicates a duplicity in connection with the qualities of the line [Fig. 3 Plate II].

When the fork is reduplicated so as to form a tassel at the end of the line, the indication is bad, denoting feebleness and nervous palpitation of the organ represented [Fig. 4 Plate II].

All branches rising from a line increase its good indications. Whereas all descending branches accentuate its bad qualities. Ascending branches indicate richness, abundance of the qualities appertaining to a line; thus on the line of heart they denote warmth of affection and devotion; on the line of head they denote cleverness and intelligence; on the line of Saturn they denote good luck, and so on. These branches, when present, are nearly always found at the beginnings and endings of lines [Fig. 5 Plate II].

## Chained & Wavy Lines

A chained formation of a line indicates obstacles, struggles, and contrarieties of the characteristics afforded by it [Fig. 6 Plate II].

A wavy formation [Fig. 7 Plate II] of a line signifies ill-luck, as does also a break in it. Breaks may be either simple interruptions or cessations of the line, or bars across it: they are always a bad sign, and the interrupting influence must be carefully sought [Fig. 8 Plate II].

When a line, instead of being single and clear, is composed of a number of little capillaries, which here and there, or at the ends unite to form a single line, it betrays obstacles and illsuccess, in the same way as chained lines [Plate II., Fig. 9].

I have gone into these general principles at this point, because it can never be too early to point them out. The reader will understand them better, however, if he will return to them after a perusal of the two succeeding sub-sections.

## Clairvoyance

Highly developed with the "Croix Mystique," well traced in the hand, and

13

pointed fingers, we find invariably a wonderful faculty of clairvoyance, which may be marvellously developed and cultivated.

I have remarked above that this mount indicates idleness; the idleness betrayed in a character by the development of this mount must not be confused with the idleness indicated by softness of the hands, the latter denoting idleness of the body, and slothfulness, as opposed to the idleness indicated by the former, which is that of the mind [reflection, etc.].

Note.—It sometimes occurs that there is a difficulty in determining the exact boundaries of the Mount of the Moon. It may generally be assumed that it joins the Mount of Mars at the extremity of the line of head, and is separated from the Triangle and the Plain of Mars by either the line of Saturn, or of Health, or by the Via Lasciva [which is rarely found in a hand].

One line upon the mount betrays a vivid instinct, a curious vague presentiment of evils; many lines rays on the mount denote visions, presentiments, prophetic dreams, and the like. Such subjects are much prone to folly and inconstancy. A single deep ray across the mount, with a small line crossing it, denotes gout or a gouty tendency.

A subject in whose hand is found a clear strong line from the Rascette to the middle of the mount [as at b, in Plate III] will be a complaining, fretful person.

A line extending in an arc from the Mount of Mercury to the Mount of the Moon, [as at a, in Plate III,] with more or less developed rays upon the mount, is an invariably sure sign of presentiments, prophetic instincts, and dreams.

Horizontal lines traced upon the percussion at the side of the Mount of the Moon denote voyages. Such a travel line terminating with, or interrupted by, a star, indicates that the voyage will be a dangerous, if not a fatal one. If a travel line be so prolonged over the Mount of the Moon into the hand as to cut the line of head, making there a star, the subject will suddenly abandon his position and prospects in life, for the sake of a perilous voyage.

A star upon the mount connected by a small line with the line of life, is a prediction of hysteria and madness [c c, in Plate III.] when it is accompanied by the other signs of dementia in a hand.

A straight line from the Mount of Mercury to that to the Moon betokens good fortune, arising from the imagination and guiding instinct developed in the mount.

## Indications of Cross-Barred Mount

The mount much cross-barred indicates a condition of constant self-torment and worry, the cause of which will be shown by some strong development elsewhere in the hand, as, for instance, by a development of the line of heart, which shows that the self-torment is from too much affection; or by a raying of the Mount of Jupiter, which shows ambition to be the disturbing element; or by a like condition of the Mount of Mercury, which indicates that the worries arise from business or commerce. This worrying tendency may, however, be counteracted by very square fingers, or a long phalanx of logic; or it may be annulled by the resistance and resignation of a high Mount of Mars.

An angle on the mount [d, in Plate III] indicates a great danger of drowning. A crescent in the same place is said to betoken the fatal influence of women upon one's life. I have not come across these signs in practice.

If in a hand the Mounts of Moon and Mercury are equally developed, it is a sign of subtilty, changeability, and intuition in the deeper sciences, bringing, as their consequence, success and even celebrity. A like combination of the mount with that of Venus results in devotion of a romantic and fantastic kind, curiosity and fastidiousness in affairs of the heart. In a bad hand such a combination will give caprice, eccentricity, and unnatural instincts in affairs of the heart. A combination with Saturn will give hypochondria and cowardice, egotism, slovenliness, and a tendency to indigestion. The constant attribute of the mount is imagination and fancy.

# Plate III

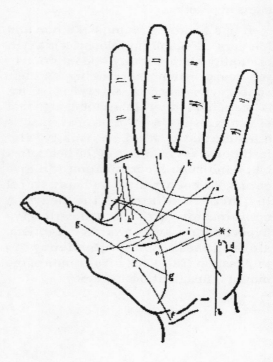

# Lines upon the Mounts of the Palm

# CHAPTER TWO

## GENERAL PRINCIPLES TO BE BORNE IN MIND

### The Mounts

The mount, which is the highest in the hand, will [as we shall see] give the keynote to the character of the subject, and will be the first thing sought for; and when the characteristics are thus pronounced by the development of a particular mount, the lesser [but still noticeable] development of another mount will indicate that the characteristics of the lesser will influence those of the greater, modifying, and in a manner perfecting, those of the reigning development.

You will seldom find that a subject has only one mount developed, and you must bear in mind in all cases that the modifying characteristics must be considered in reading the primary indications of the principal mount.

A characteristic betrayed by a prevailing mount can never lie dormant in a subject; opportunities for exercising the qualities indicated will always arise, for the subject will, in a way, make them himself —e.g., a man whose leading mount is that of Mars will, by provoking others, call the talents of his character into play.

If a subject has no particularly prominent mount in his hand—i.e., all the mounts are equal—you will find a singular regularity of mind and harmony of existence to be his lot.

If all the mounts are null, and the places where they should be are merely occupied by a plain or a hollow, you will find that the subject has never had any opportunity of developing any particular characteristic, and the life will be a purely vegetative one.

A mount may, instead of being high, be broad and full, or it may be covered with little lines. These conditions of the mount give it the same effect as if it were highly developed; and it must be remarked that, if a mount is much covered by lines, it will betray an excess and overabundance of the qualities of the mount, which prove an insurmountable obstacle to the good effects thereof. Excess of a mount does not give force, but fever to its quality, producing monomanias, especially if the thumb and the line of head are weak.

## Lines on a mount

**One** line upon a mount just emphasizes it enough to be a fortunate sign upon it; **two** lines show uncertainty in the operation of the qualities, especially if they are crossed; and **three**, except in some rare cases, give misfortune arising from the qualities of the mount, unless they be even, straight, and parallel. If no other mount is developed, the one upon which most lines are found will be the leading mount in the hand.

Lines placed **crosswise** upon a mount always denote obstacles, and seriously interfere with the goodness of other main lines, which end upon the mount, as in the cases of the mounts and lines of Saturn, or of Apollo, unless the ascending line is deeper than the cross lines, in which case the evil indications of the cross lines are destroyed.

De Peruchio affirms that little capillary cross lines upon a mount signify wounds; thus on the Mount of Jupiter they signify a wound to the head; on that of Saturn, to the breast; on that of Apollo, to the arms; on that of Mercury, to the legs; on that of Venus, to the body. I have encountered some strange confirmations of this statement, but such instances are rare.

Thus it will be seen that the indications afforded by any particular mount may be greatly modified, if not annulled, by the appearance of lines upon it, or in its immediate vicinity, so that these must be carefully sought for and examined concomitantly.

It will be very frequently found that the mounts are not exactly under the fingers, but lean, as it were, in the direction of the neighbouring mount. In such cases the prevailing development takes a modification from that towards which it inclines.

## Good or bad influences of a Mount

Finally, the influence of the mount, which is principally developed, may be either good or bad. Desbarrolles has stated that this may be determined by the expression of the face, but I think by far the surer and more scientific determination may be arrived at by inspecting the formation of the tips of the fingers, the consistency of the hand, and the development of the thumb. Thus, pointed fingers reveal an intuition, a lofty idealism of the quality. Square fingers will look at the reasonable aspects of character, and spatulate will cultivate the *material* qualities of the mount—e.g., Jupiter developed will indicate, with pointed fingers, religion; with square fingers, pride; and with spatulate fingers, tyranny. Apollo developed will indicate, with pointed fingers, love of glory; with square fingers, realism in art; and with spatulate fingers, love of wealth and luxury. And so on with the other mounts.

Most authors have gone into the phrenology and physiognomy characteristic of each type, but as I consider this to be not only confusing, but irrelevant to the study of pure cheiromancy, I have avoided the consideration of this matter.

The lines in a hand should be clear and apparent. They should be neat and well coloured [not broad and pale], free from branches, breaks, inequalities, or modifications of any sort, except in some few cases, which will be pointed out in due course. A broad pale line always signifies [by indicating excess] a defect of, and obstacle to, the natural indications and qualities of the line.

Pale lines signify a phlegmatic or lymphatic temperament, with a strong tendency towards effeminacy [women nearly always have very pale lines]. Such subjects are easily put out, and as easily calmed again; they are generally liberal, and subject to strong enthusiasms, which are of short duration.

Red lines indicate a sanguine temperament, and are good; such subjects are gay, pleasant in manner, and honest.

Yellow lines denote biliousness and feebleness of the liver; such subjects are quick-tempered, prompt in action, generally ambitious, vigilant, vindictive, and proud.

## The Mounts of the Hands

I have already indicated where the various mounts should be placed. The prevailing mount is the first thing to be observed in the palm of a hand, and it must be sought for with a careful regard to the general principles laid down in the section "General Principles To Be Borne in Mind." In this subsection we shall carefully consider the indications afforded by each mount in succession, as well as those of some of the principal combinations of mounts.

## The Mount of Jupiter

The predominance of this mount in a hand denotes a genuine and reverential feeling of religion, a worthy and high ambition, honour, gaiety, and a love of nature. It also denotes a love of display, of ceremony, and of pomp, and is, consequently, generally developed in the hands of public entertainers of any sort. Such subjects talk loudly, are extremely self-confident, are just and well-minded, gallant and extravagant, and are always impetuous without being revengeful. These subjects are fond of flattery and fond of good living. They generally marry early, and are always well-built and handsome, having a certain *hauteur*, which enhances their charms without detracting from their good nature.

An excessive development of the mount will give arrogance, tyranny, ostentation, and, with pointed fingers, superstition. Such subjects will be votaries of pleasure, and vindictive, sparing nothing to attain their selfish ends.

If the mount is absent [i.e., replaced by a cavity] the subject is prone to idleness and egoism, irreligious feelings, want of dignity and a license which degenerates into vulgarity.

The development of this mount gives to square fingers a great love of regularity and established authority. To long smooth fingers it imparts a love of luxury, especially if the fingers are large at the third phalanx. This mount ought always to be accompanied by a smooth, elastic, firm hand [not too hard], with a well-developed first phalanx to the thumb [Will].

## Influence of Saturn

If to the good indications of this mount a favorably developed finger, or Mount of Saturn, be added, the success in life and good fortune of the subject is certain; Saturn denoting fatality, whether for good or evil.

A single line upon the mount indicates success. Many and confused lines upon the mount betray a constant, unsuccessful struggle for greatness, and if these confused lines are crossed, they denote promiscuousness, no matter the sex of the subject.

A cross upon the mount denotes a happy marriage, and if a star be found there as well as the cross, it indicates a brilliant and advantageous alliance.

A spot upon the mount indicates a fall of position, and loss of honour or credit.

A long thumb and a development of the first joint in the fingers will give to this mount free thought and irreverence in religion. If besides these, we find pointed fingers and what is called the "Croix Mystique," you will find ecstasy in matters religious, tending even to fanaticism.

If, instead of being in position immediately underneath the fingers of Jupiter, [or forefinger,] the mount is displaced and inclines towards that of Saturn, it acquires a serious tone and demeanour, and gives a desire for success in science, theology, or classical scholarship. If with the Mount of Jupiter we find also the Mount of Apollo developed, it indicates good fortune and wealth. Combined with the Mount of Mercury we find a love of exact science and philosophy. Such subjects are inclined to be poetic, are well behaved and clever; they make the most successful doctors. To a bad hand this combination will give vanity, egoism, a love of chatter, fanaticism, charlatanry, and immorality. Combined with the Mount of Mars it gives audacity and the talent of strategy. Such subjects self-confident, successful, and fond of celebrity. To a bad hand such a combination gives insolence, ferocity, revolt, dissipation, and inconstancy. A combination of the Mounts of Jupiter and of the Moon makes a subject honourable, palcid, and just. With the Mount of Venus a subject of this Jupiterian type becomes sociable, simple-minded, gay, sincere, fond of pleasure, and generous. If the hand is, on the whole, bad, the combination will denote effeminacy, feeble-mindedness, caprice, and a love of debauchery.

## The Mount of Saturn

The predominance of this mount in a hand denotes a character in which to prudence and natural caution is added a fatality for good or evil, which is extreme. By fatality is meant *certainty,* i.e., the indications of the middle finger are always looked upon as certain and unavoidable; and we find a curious parallel to this in comparative anatomy by observing the greater *constancy* of this finger: i.e., the fact that it is the one digit that is never discarded in the brute creation. Professor Owen calls attention to this, in his work "On the Nature of Limbs" [p. 38], where he points out the fact that the extreme digits [the thumb and little finger] are the least constant and universal, whilst the "digitus medius" is the most constant of all in the vertebrate series, and most entitled to be viewed as the persistent representative of the *fingers;* it shows a superiority of size, though few would be led thereby to suspect that the bones forming the three joints of this finger answer to those of the foot of the horse, and that the *nail* of this finger represents the *hoof* in the horse, etc.

Such subjects are always sensitive and particular about little things, even though their fingers be short. The mount also denotes a tendency to occult science, to incredulity, and to epicureanism temperament. Such subjects are always inclined to be morbid and melancholy. They are timid, and love solitude, and a quiet life in which there is neither great good fortune nor great ill fortune; they are also fonder of serious music than of gay melody. They take naturally to such pursuits as agriculture, horticulture, or mineralogy, having a natural penchant for anything connected with the earth. These subjects seldom marry, are extremely self-centered and self-confident, and care nothing for what other people may think of them.

The mount is seldom very high, for fatality is always, to a certain extent, modifiable; but when there is an excess of formation on this mount it betrays taciturnity, sadness, an increased morbidity and love of solitude, remorse, and asceticism, with the horrible opposing characteristics of an intense fear and horror of death, with a morbid tendency to, and curiosity concerning suicide. The evil indications of an excessive development may be greatly modified by a well-formed Mount of Venus.

# Saturnian Hand

The Saturnian hand has generally long, bony fingers, which give it philosophy, the second finger [that of Saturn] is large, with the first [or nailed] phalanx highly developed, the mount, if not high, being generally strongly lined. A bad Saturnian hand has a hard rough skin and a thick wrist.

If the mount is quite absent the indication is of an insignificant, "vegetable" existence, unmoved by any great depth of feeling, and one which is continually oppressed by a sense of misfortune. But when it is thus absent it may be replaced by a well-traced line of fate [or Saturn].

A single straight line upon the mount signifies good fortune and success, whilst a plurality of lines thereon indicates a proportionate ill-luck. A succession of little lines placed ladder-wise across the mount and extending upon that of Jupiter indicate an easy and gradual progression to high honour.

A spot upon the mount always indicates an evil fatality, the cause of which must be sought for upon the lines of head or of fate.

If a branch [not the end of the line of heart or of Saturn] rises from the line of heart on to the Mount of Saturn, it denotes worry, travail, and anxiety; if the branch is clean and single however, it will foreshadow wealth as a result of those anxieties [*l*, in Plate III].

If, instead of being in its proper position beneath the second finger, the mount is displaced towards Jupiter, it has the same significance as the displacement of the Mount of Jupiter towards Saturn. If, on the other hand, it is displaced towards the Mount of Apollo, it betokens a fatality which can be, and must be, striven against.

If, together with the Mount of Saturn, we find the Mount of Jupiter developed, we shall find gentleness, patience, and respect in a good hand, or want of appreciation, inability to make use of opportunities, melancholy, hysteria, and want of taste in a bad hand. Combined with that of Mercury this mount gives us antiquarian research, and love of science from an "amateur" point of view, a talent for medicine, and a desire for information

# Plate III

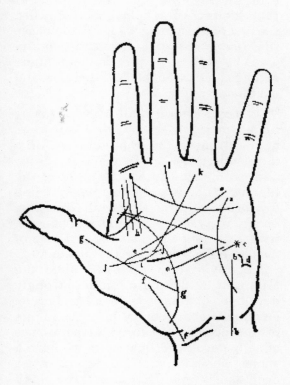

## Lines upon the Mounts of the Palm

on various subject. Such subjects are clever at individualizing and classing, and are generally happy. And this latter indication generally holds good even when the rest of the hand is bad, in which case the combination of Saturn and Mercury gives us perfidy, perjury, sullen temper, revenge, theft, want of filial affection, and charlatanry.

With the Mount of Mars equally developed this mount betokens aggressiveness, bitterness of humour, a false superiority, insolence, immodesty, and cynicism. The combination of the Mounts of Venus and Saturn will give us a love of and a search after truth in matters occult, piety, charity, logic, self control, with a tendency to jealousy and love of display. If the hand is bad the combination will betray frivolity, curiosity, and, if the Mount of Saturn be the more strongly developed of the two, we shall find pride, envy, and debauchery. When the Mounts of the Moon and of Saturn find themselves equally developed in a hand, we have a subject whose intuition and pure talent for occultism is remarkably developed. It is a curious fact that these latter subjects are generally frightfully ugly.

## The Mount of Apollo

A hand in which this mount is developed is essentially that of a subject whose prevailing tastes and instincts are artistic, and it always gives to its possessor a greater or a lesser degree of success, glory, celebrity, and brilliancy of fortune, denoting, as it does, genius, intelligence, tolerance, and wealth, the characteristics of the type being self-confidence, beauty, grace, and tolerance in all things.

Such subjects are inventive and imitative, being often great discoverers. Their principal failings are, quick temper [though not of long duration] and a certain incapacity for very close friendships, though they are generally benevolent and generous, even devoted were it not for the inseparable strain of fickleness. Proud and eloquent on matters of art, they love anything which is brilliant, such as jewelry and the more ornamental forms of worship, for they are religious from a gratitude for blessings received rather than from a superstitious reverence. They make stern and unrelenting judges, and their love is more affectionate than sensual.

These Apollonian subjects love to shine before the world, and not to be the cynosures of a small circle of admirers, though they hate the idea of ostentation or undeserved glory; they will not explain themselves in dogmatizing unless they think their audiences are sympathetic, refusing to waste words on ignorant cavillers, or to persuade people to accept their opinions. In marriage they are, unfortunately, very often unlucky, for their ideal, their standard of excellence, is unreasonably high.

## Apollonian Hand

The normal development of a hand bearing this mount high shows smooth fingers, with the tips mixed or slightly squared; the palm of an equal length with the fingers, a well marked phalanx of logic, and either one very deep, or three strong lines upon the mount.

If the mount is developed to excess it indicates a love of wealth and of extravagance in expenditure, instincts of luxury, fatuity, envy, and curiosity, a quick, unreasoning temper, and a strong tendency to levity, frivolity, and sophistry. Such subjects are boastful, vain, think themselves unappreciated, but highly superior to their fellow-men; these are the poets, painters, and musicians and actors who dwell upon the loss suffered by the world in their non-appearance at St. James's Hall, Burlington House, and the Lyceum. This excessive development is generally accompanied, and is emphasized by twisted fingers, spatulated soft hands, a grille on the mount, with a long phalanx of will and proportionately short phalanx of logic.

If on the other hand, this mount is absent in both hands, its absence betrays materiality and indifference to matters artistic, giving a dull, unenlightened life.

A single line deeply traced upon the mount indicates fortune and glory; two lines indicate considerable talent, but a great probability of failure, whilst many confused lines show a tendency to lean to the scientific aspects of art.

If the mount is merely developed, having no line marked upon it, it shows a love of the beautiful, but not necessarily a talent for production of works of art.

A spot upon the mount denotes a grave danger of a loss of reputation or caste.

## Combination of Apollo and Moon

When in a hand the Mounts of Apollo and of Mercury are found equally developed, we find a character in which justice, firmness, perspicacity, love of scientific research, features. The combination of Apollo and the Moon gives good sense, imagination, reflection, and light-heartedness. With an equal development of the Mount of Venus, we get amiability and a great desire to please.

## The Mount of Mercury

The pre-eminence in a hand of this mount indicates science, intelligence, spirit, eloquence, a capacity for commerce, speculation, industry, and invention, agility, promptitude in thought and action, and a penchant for travel and occult science.

The eloquence, which is one of the prevailing characteristics of the type, is of a kind denoted by the formations of the fingers. A high Mount of Mercury will give, with pointed fingers, brilliant oratory; with square fingers, clearness and reason in expounding; with spatulate fingers, force and vehemence in argument and dogma; with long fingers, details and parentheses; and with short fingers, brevity and conciseness. The great difference between the eloquence of these subjects, and of those whose prevailing mount is that of Apollo, is that the oratory of the former is sophistical and clever, rather than naïve and direct like that of the latter; it is this that makes them such good barristers. To assist their faculties in this respect still further, these subjects should always have short nails.

## Indications of the Mount

Such subjects are good athletes, are agile, clever at games of skill, spontaneous and expedient, sharp in practice, with a great capacity for serious studies. Combined with these qualities we generally recognise envy, but amiability therewith; often [the other conditions of the hand being favourable] we find that these subjects are clever clairvoyants, seldom sensual, and generally good-humoured, and fond of playing with children so long as they are not otherwise seriously employed. This tendency to envy, by raising envious feelings at the aptitudes and successes of others, constantly drives these Mercurial subjects to take up and try a great variety of pursuits.

These subjects are great match-makers, and frequently marry very young, choosing equally young persons for their helpmates.

The normal development of the hand which accompanies this mount is as follows:— Long, smooth fingers, hard, slightly spatulated, [athletics,] or very soft with mixed tips [thought]. The finger of Mercury long and sometimes pointed. The high mount cut by a deep line, and the philosophic joint developed.

If the mount is developed to excess in a hand, it denotes theft, cunning, deceit, treachery, with pretentious ignorance. Such subjects are charlatans, running after the false and dishonest forms of occultism, and are generally superstitious. These hands usually have long twisted fingers, more or less turned back; soft hands, confused markings on the mount, and the phalanx of will long.

A complete absence of the mount denotes inaptitude for science or for commercial enterprise.

A single line upon the mount indicates modesty and moderation, and in many instances a strange unexpected stroke of good fortune. A cross line extening upon the Mount of Apollo betrays charlatanry in science, and, in fact, the dishonest occultism I have alluded to above. If this line has an "island" in it and cuts the Line of Apollo or brilliancy, it denotes ill-luck, probably resulting from some perfectly innocent act.

Many mixed lines upon the mount denote astuteness and aptitude for sciences. If they reach as low as the line of heart, they denote liberality; and if to numerous rays on this mount a subject joints a high Mount of the Moon, his penchant for medical science will take the form of hypochondria. The elder cheiromants have affirmed that a woman having this mount well rayed is sure to marry a doctor, or, at any rate, a man of science. If the lines on the mount merely take the form of little flecks and dashes, it is a sure indication of a babbling, chattering disposition.

## Lines of the side of the Head

Lines on the percussion—i.e., on the edge of the hand, between the base of the little finger and the line of heart—indicate liaisons, or serious affairs of the heart if horizontal, [i.e., parallel with the line of the heart,] each line denoting a separate liaison or love affair, a single deep line denoting one strong and lasting affection. If vertical they denote, almost invariably, the number of children which the subject has had. De Peruchio lays down the rule that if they are strong they denote boys, if faint, girls; and if they are short or indistinct the children are either dead or not yet born. Several vertical lines on the percussion, crossed by a line which starts from a star on the percussion, crossed by a line which starts from a star upon the mount, betrays sterility, whilst a marriage line, ending abruptly in a star, indicates a marriage or liaison of short duration, terminated by death.

The mount quite smooth and unlined indicates a cool, determined, and constant condition of mind. A grille upon the mount is a dangerous prognostic of a violent death, a circle also placed upon the mount indicating that it will be by water. A spot upon the mount indicates an error or misfortune in business.

If the mount is high, and the hand contains a long line of Apollo, the commercial instinct will work itself out in speculation rather than in recognized and persevering commerce.

The mount leaning, as it were, towards that of Apollo, is a good sign, good enough to counteract a bad line of Saturn, betokening science and eloquence. Leaning in a contrary direction [i.e., towards the percussion,] it indicates commerce and industry.

Connected with the Mount of Venus by a good line, [i.e., in Plate III] this mount gives happiness and good fortune.

Combined [i.e., equally developed] with the Mount of Venus, we find wit, humour, gaiety, love of beauty, often piety, easy and sympathetic eloquence. In a bad hand [i.e., if the fingers are twisted, the line of head weak, and the phalanx of will small] this combination will give inconsequence, contradiction, meddlesomeness, inconstancy, and want of perseverance. The combination of Mercury and Saturn in a hand is always good, giving to the sobriety and fatality of Saturn, a certain intuitive practicality which seldom fails to give good results. The mount of Mercury is, however, one which is not often combined with the other mounts of the hand.

# The Mount of Mars

The discussion of the Mount of Mars is not fraught with that simplicity which characterises that of the other mounts. It is, in a manner, divided into the Mount of Mars properly so called, which is situated, as may be seen, beneath the Mount of Mercury on the percussion into the palm of the hand [shown in Plate I. by a dagger] which is known as the Plain of Mars. It will be seen that a development of the Mount of Mars becomes the Plain of Mars, by the swelling it produces in that part of the palm occupied by the Triangle; and as the Plain of Mars is treated of in my remarks upon the triangle, but little notice need be taken of it here. The keynote of the whole question may be struck by bearing in mind that the Mount of Mars denotes resistance, whereas the Plain of Mars betrays action and aggression. This will be more fully demonstrated later on.

The main characteristics indicated by a development of the Mount of Mars are courage, calmness, sang-froid in moments of emergency, resignation in misfortune, pride, resolution, resistance, and devotion, with a strong capacity to command.

Well developed and not covered by lines or rays, this mount will counteract the evil influences of a short thumb by the calmness and resignation which it imparts to a character. Such a subject [especially if his thumb be large] possesses, to a marked extent, the capacity for keeping his temper. He will be magnanimous and generous to extravagance, loud of voice, and hot-blooded, his passions carrying him even to sensuality, unless counteracted by a strong phalanx of logic. His eloquence, if he possess that faculty, rare among subjects of this type, will be of the fascinating rather than of the emotional description. Spatulate fingers will give to this mount a love of show and self-glory.

These subjects have always a great natural inclination to love, though they nearly always marry late in life, and marry women of the type of Venus. These two types seem to have a natural inclination for one another. "I know not how, but martial men are given to love. I think it is but as they are given to wine; for perils commonly asked to be paid is pleasures." FRACIS BACON'S "Essay on Love," 1612.

## Aspects of the Hand

The hands to which these martial mounts belong are generally hard, the fingers large, especially at the third phalanx, the will long, and the logic small, the hollow of the hand [Plain of Mars] rayed and lined.

An excessive development of this mount, [i.e., a spreading of the mount into the palm, "the Plain of Mars,"] or a mass of lines upon the mount, will indicate brusquerie, fury, injustice of mind, insolence, violence, cruelty, blood-thirstiness, insult, and defiance of manner. Lines on the mount always denote hot temper. This excessive development generally betrays lasciviousness, and exaggeration in speech.

The Plain of Mars highly developed or covered with lines indicates a love of contest, struggle, and war, especially if the nails be short and a cross be found in the plain. This network of little lines in the Plain of Mars always indicates obstacles in the way of real good fortune.

These hands of the excessive type have generally a feeble line of heart often joined to the line of head, the line of life red in colour, and the thumb short and clubbed.

If the mount be completely absent, its absence denotes cowardliness and childishness.

De Peruchio and Tainsnier both assert that a line extending from the Mount of Mars to between the Mounts of Jupiter and Saturn, with little spots on the line of head, indicate deafness. I have never recognized the sign.

Combined with the Mount of Apollo, this mount becomes an indication of ardour and energy in art, force, perseverance, and truth in action. With the Mount of the Moon we get a love of anvigation, or, if the rest of the hand is bad, folly. Combined with the Mount of Venus we find a love of music and of dancing, sensuality, ardour, and jealousy in love. The combination of Mars and mercury denotes movement and quickness of thought and speech, spontaneity, incredulity, and a love of argument, strife of words, and mockery. An equal development of the Mounts of Saturn and Mars gives cynicism, audacity of belief and opinion, and want of moral sense; we find, in fact, in this case, the energy of Mars rousing to action the usually letent evil qualities of Saturn.

## The Mount of the Moon

The attributes of this mount, when found predominant in a hand, are imagination, melancholy, chastity, poetry of soul, and a love of mystery, solitude, and silence, with a tendency to reverie and imagination. To it belongs also the domain of harmony in music, as opposed to the melody, which is the special attribute [as we shall see] of the Mount of Venus.

Such subjects are generally capricious and changeable, egoists, and inclined to be idle; their imagination often makes them hypochondriacal, and their abstraction often causes them to develop the faculty of presentiment, giving them intuition, prophetic instincts, and dreams. They are fond of voyages by reason of their restlessness, they are more mystic than religious, phlegmatic in habit, fantastic, and given to romance in matters of art and literature. They make generally the best rhymists, but they have no self-confidence, no perseverance, and no powers of expression in speech. They are much given to capricious marriages, which astonish their friends, from disparity of years, or something of the kind.

These hands are generally swollen and soft, with short, smooth, and pointed fingers, and a short phalanx of logic. For the influence of the mount to be altogether good, it should be fuller at the base [near the wrist] then at the top [near the Mount of Mars] or in the centre. Excessive fullness in the exact centre generally betrays some internal or intestinal weakness whilst excessive fullness at the top indicates, as a rule, biliousness, goutiness, and a susceptibility to catarrh. Bad concomitant signs are a forking of the head line, a low Mount of Mars, with the Mount of Apollo covered with a grille; then we find betrayed the vices of slander, debauchery, immodesty, insolence, and cowardice.

The mount developed with a hard hand often betokens a dangerous activity and exercise of the imagination; with spatulate fingers this subject will be constantly forming projects and plans.

## Effect of Finger Tips

It may well be understood that a development of this mount emphasizes and harmonizes admirably with pointed fingers, but its development makes a square-fingered subject miserable by the constant turmoil and struggle between the realms of fact and fancy, unless there appears in the hand a good and well-traced line of Apollo, which will give an artistic turn and instinct to the regularity of the square fingers. But if the fingers of the hand which bears this mount be very long. Or very square, the inevitable result will be a perpetual discontent.

A development of this hand should always be accompanied by short fingers, otherwise the detail indicated by the fingers will be constantly fretting the let-go instincts of the mount, or the morbid imagination of the mount will turn the detail of the fingers into a positive disease.

An excessive development of the Mount of the Moon will produce in a character unregulated caprice, wild imaginations, irritability, discontent, sadness, superstition, fanaticism, and error. Such subjects are intensely liable to suffer from headaches; and they take a morbid pleasure in painful thoughts and humiliating reflections.

When the mount is not high, but very long, coming down to the base of the hand, and forming an angle with the wrist, it denotes a resigned and contemplative character, quite devoid of all strength, being shown by thickness, as opposed to weakness, which is indicated by the length of the mount.

If the mount is absolutely absent, it betrays want of ideas and imagination, want of poetry of mind, and general drought of the intellect.

## The Mount of Venus

The main attributes of this mount, shown in a character by its prominence in the hand, are the possession of, and an admiration for, beauty, grace, melody in music, dancing, gallantry, tenderness, and benevolence, with a constant desire to please and to be appreciated. It is essentially the Mount of Melody, and is, consequently, always to be found in the hands of those who are talented as singers. The attributes of this mount are the more feminine forms of beauty, as contrasted with the masculine forms of beauty, which are indicated by prominence of the Mount of Jupiter.

These subjects are great lovers of pleasure and society; they are fond of applause, but more from their love of giving pleasure to others than for its own sake. They hate any form of quarrel or strife, and are essentially gay, though they are less noisily gay, as a rule, than subjects of the type of Jupiter. [See above]. Men of the type are often effeminate; all of them, however, have the talents of painting, poetry, and music, whether they have the perseverance to cultivate them or not.

A development of this mount will always mitigate and soften the harsh effects, or malignities, of any other mount.

The hand which usually accompany a development of this mount are fat and dimpled, the fingers smooth and rather short, the thumb also short. The bad influence of the type is betrayed by extreme softness, pointed fingers, the mount much cross-barred, the line of Mars indicated inside the line of life, and the Via Lasciva traced upon the palm.

An excess of the mount will betray debauchery, effrontery, license, inconstancy, vanity, flirtation, and levity.

The absence of the mount betrays coldness, laziness, and dullness in matters of art. Without this mount developed to a certain extent, all the other passions become dry and selfish in their action.

If the mount is completely devoid of lines, it indicates coldness, chastity, and, very often a short life.

A quantity of lines on the mount denotes always heat of passion and warmth of temperament. If there are but two or three strong lines traced upon the mount, they indicate ingratitude.

A worn-out libertine has always this mount flat, but very much rayed, the Girdle of Venus being also traced in the hand, which indicates that the desire of the subject being beyond his powers, he constantly seeks for change and new excitement.

A line extending from the mount to that of Mercury [e e, in Plate III] is always a good sign, indicating good fortune and love resulting from one another.

A line rising from the base of the hand into the mount is also a sign of good luck [ff, in Plate III]

## Marriage Hands

Lines from the phalanx of logic to the line of life [gg, in Plate III] are said by many authorities to indicate marriages; and if they are confused, betray troubles and worries in love and marriage.

Islands placed crosswise upon the mount [j j, in Plate III] indicate advantageous opportunities of marriage which have been missed. These lost opportunities would have been all the more brilliant and desirable if the islands are connected with the Mount of Apollo [as at k, in Plate III] by a line.

Three lines extending straight to the Mount of Jupiter denote liberality and happiness [h h, in Plate III]. A deep line cutting into the triangle [i i, in Plate III] betrays a tendency to asthma.

Note. -- It has been an almost invariable rule among cheirosophists to make these mounts the bases and distinguishing characteristics of seven clearly defined types, assigning to each a special physiognomy, phrenology, etc. I do not consider that this is expedient, for hands are already divided into seven far more practical and ordinary types cheirognomically, and in all my experience I have never found more than five or six subjects whose hands were dominated by one single pre-eminent mount.

# Plate IV

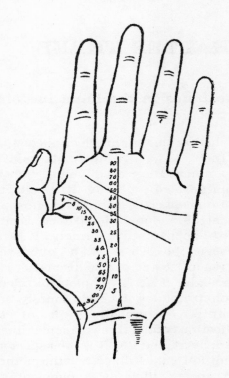

**Age upon the Lines of Life and Fortune**

# CHAPTER THREE

## The Lines in the hand in detail

I shall consider and discuss each line in turn, according to its relative importance. The great difficulty about the consideration of the lines in the acquirement of the dogma of cheirosophy, is that the amount of detail to be learnt by heart is apparently enormous. It is not, however, the case, as will be found when we reach the end of this discussion, for, as a matter of fact, a complete knowledge of cheiromancy depends merely on a complete comprehension of the indications of the three principal lines - head, heart, and life. It is the aspect and condition of these lines, and the methods and causes of their disarrangements and subdivisions, which, properly observed, afford us all the information we can possibly require.

# The Line of Life

This line should be long, completely encircling the ball of the thumb [Mount of Venus], strong, not too broad or too fine, without curvature, breakage, cross bars, or irregularities of any description. Thus marked in a hand, it denotes long life, good health, a good character and disposition.

Pale and broad, it indicates ill-health, bad instincts, and a feeble and envious character. Thick and red, it betrays violence and brutality of mind; chained, [vide fig. 6, Plate II.,] it indicates delicacy of constitution; thin and meagre in the centre, it indicates ill-health during a portion of the life; a spot terminating this thinness indicates sudden death. If it is of various thicknesses throughout its course it denotes a capricious and fickle temper.

Perhaps the most important consideration connected with this line is the determination of age. The line is divided up into periods of five and ten years, in the manner shown in Plate IV and according as irregularities or breaks occur at any of these points, an illness or event whatsoever threatens the life at that age. [Thus, for instance, say a break occurs on a line of life at the point where you see the figure 40, you may predict an illness at that age or say the line ceases abruptly at the point 55, you may predict the death of the subject at that age...]. It has often been objected to me that it is difficult to divide the line in a living hand from a diagram like Plate IV., owing to the difference in the size; but the difficulty ought not to exist, for the circumference of the Mount of Venus has only to be divided [mentally] into eighteen equal parts, the points of division of which should be taken to represent the ages indicated on the diagram. A little experience will render this mental operation quite easy. The Plate VII. As given in Adrien Desbarrolles' smaller work on the science has led many would be cheirosophists wide of the mark, for the divisions are impracticable and incorrect, and his treatment of the other lines in the same way, by rays from the line of life, is hopelessly and physically impossible. The method in which this division was obtained, and the astrological reasons and explanation thereof are given at length at p. 236 of the same work, but they are too lengthy and useless to transcribe here. He himself has recognized the fallacy of this method and subdivision, and hastens to correct them in the very first words of his later and larger work, where he gives a diagram practically identical with Plate IV, as regards the divisions of the line.

The shorter the line the shorter the life, and from the point at which the line terminates in both hands may be predicted accurately the time at which death will supervene.

A break in the line denotes always an illness. If the line is broken in both hands, there is great danger of death, especially if the lower branch of the break turn inwards towards the Mount of Venus [as at a, in Plate V], and the sign is repeated in both hands.

And here I would digress to impress upon my readers a point of vital importance; that is, the absolute necessity to bear in mind that to be certain a sign must be repeated in both hands; and this applies particularly and especially to the indications of accident and disease upon the line of life. A break in one hand, and not in the other, betokens only a danger of illness; and in like manner, if in one hand the line stop short at 35, death

# Plate V

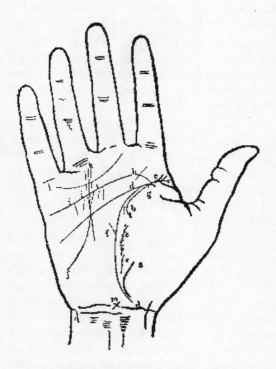

**Modifications of the Principal Lines**

cannot be predicted at that age, unless it also stop short at the same point in the other. For example, I saw a pair of hands some years since, in which the line ceased at 37 in one hand, and at 41 in the other. I told the subject that a fatal illness would attack him at 37, which would kill him at 41. He replied that he was then 39, and, as I had told him, he died two years afterwards. These things must be very carefully learnt before they are put into practice, for to make a deliberate statement like the above would be a brutal and dangerous thing to do, unless one spoke with absolute certainty.

## What Causes Sudden Death?

The line ceasing abruptly with a few little parallel lines as at *b*, in Plate V, is an indication of sudden death. If the line is continually crossed by little cutting bars, it is an indication of continual, but not severe, illnesses.

If the line is broken up and laddered, as at *c c*, in Plate V, it denotes a period of continued delicacy and ill-health. If it is broken inside a square, as at a, in Plate VI., it indicates recovery from a serious illness; a square always denotes protection from some danger. A bar across the broken ends [as at b, Plate VI] also denotes a preservation from an illness.

Whatever may be the condition of the line, a sister line, as at d d, Plate V, will replace it and counteract the evil effects of the irregularities found on the main line, protect the subject against most of the dangers which assail him, and indicate a luxurious, comfortable existence. [Of the inner sister line, or line of Mars, we shall speak later on.]

The line should be free from forks and tassels throughout its course. Tasselled at its extremity, as at c, in Plate VI, it indicates poverty and loss of money late in life, if not earlier. Forked at the commencement, as at e, Plate V, it indicates vanity, indecision, and fantasy; but if the fork is very clear and simple, [not confused as in the figure.] it may in a good hand mean justice of soul and fidelity. In like manner, if instead of the tassel at c, Plate VI., we find a plain fork, it points to overwork in old age resulting in poverty; it is, in fact, the first warning of the appearance of the tassel. A ray of the tassel going to the Mount of the Moon [as at d, Plate VI] shows a great danger of folly resulting from

# Plate VI

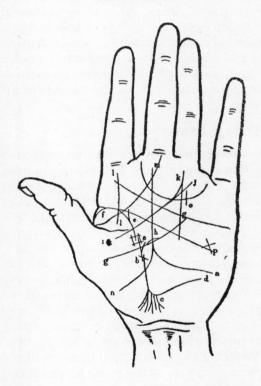

**Modifications of the Principal Lines**

these troubles. A fork going to the line of head [as at e, Plate VI] equals faithfulness, but if it be at the side of the hand as at f, it is, on the contrary, a sign of inconstancy. A fork in the very centre of the line is a warning of diminished force, which must be attended to by a relaxation of the efforts, especially if the tassel appears at the base of the line, or the head is at all weak.

## Worry Lines

Rays across the hand from the Mount of Venus [as in Plate VII] always denote worries and troubles. Across the line of fortune to a star in the triangle, they denote loss of money; continued to the line of head, as at b, a ray indicates a consequent loss of reason, or, at any rate, danger to the mental faculties. Cutting the line of Apollo, as at c, it betokens a worry or loss of money early in life, by reason of the ruin or misfortune of one's parents; if it starts from a star, as at d, it shows that the misfortune was caused by the death of a parent. The age at which these troubles occur is shown by the place at which the line of life is cut by the worry line. If the worry line terminates at a point or star upon the lines of head or heart [as from f, in Plate VII], or upon the Mount of Mars it denotes that the worry has brought about an illness. If the line goes straight to the heart, as at g g, in Plate VI, it indictes an unhappy love affair; if an island appear in the line, [h, Plate VI] the consequences are likely to be, or have been, serious, if not shameful; a fork at the point where g g cuts the line of life, as in Plate VI, indicates an unhappy marriage, or even a divorce. A worry line from a star in the mount [I, Plate VI] indicates quarrels with relations, ending in ruin if it goes up to the Mount of Apollo, as at j; but it goes up and joins with the line of Apollo, as at k, it is a prediction of good fortune arising therefrom. A line from the Mount of Venus, just cutting the line of life, as at h, in Plate VII, indicates marriage at the age whereat the line is found.

Rays across the hand just cutting the line, generally indicate an illness caused by the mount or line whence the ray takes its departure, at the age at which it occurs upon the line: thus, from the Line of Heart it means an illness caused by the head or brain; from the Mount of Mars a danger brought about by passion, and so on.

A ray ascending to the Mount of Jupiter, as at l l, in Plate VI, betrays ambition, lofty aims, egoism, and success. These lines often appear in a hand quite suddenly.

If a branch rise from a black spot on the line, it indicates that a disease has left a nervous complaint. Black spots always indicate diseases, and if they are very deep, they indicate sudden death. Among the older Cheiromants this was the indication of a murderer. These are more particularly treated of later on.

## Ascending and Descending Branches

Branches ascending from the line, as in Plate VIII, denote ambition, and nearly always riches; if they ascend *through* the other lines, as at a a a, they indicate that the success is brought about by the personal merit of the subject. *Descending* branches, as at b, Plate VIII, denote loss of health and wealth.

If instead of starting from the extreme outside of the hand, the line of life commences under the Mount of Jupiter, [say at g, Plate V], it betrays great ambition, and is often a sign of great successes and honours.

# Plate VII

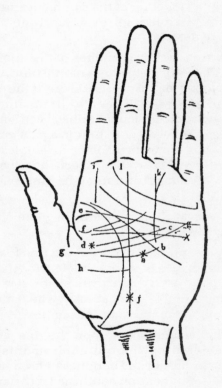

# Modifications of the Principal Lines

If the lines of life, head, and heart are all joined together at the commencement, it is a terrible sign of misfortune and violent death.

A cross cut by branches of the line, as at c, Plate VIII, betokens a mortal infirmity, with grave fear of death; a cross at the end of the line, as at d, denotes [if the line is otherwise clear] that the subject will suffer unmerited reverses in his old age. A cross at the commencement of the line indicates an accident in early life, especially if a point be also found on the line at the same place.

A line from the Mount of Mars cutting the line of life, as at e e, in Plate VIII, indicates a wound.

A ray going direct from the line to the Mount of Apollo, denotes celebrity; if it is indistinct, this celebrity is obstructed by some quality of the character, which must be sought for and guarded against.

Circles and spots upon the line were considered by the old cheiromants to indicate murder and blindness. I have seen the latter indication confirmed, but never the former.

If the line, instead of being joined to the line of head, be separated, as at f, in

Plate VIII., it is a sign of folly and carelessness, of extreme self-reliance and foolhardiness in consequence, especially if the space be filled with a mesh of little lines, and the lines themselves be big and red.

If the lines come out in a great circle into the palm of the hand, and reach, or end close to, the Mount of the Moon, it is a sign of long life. As I have said before, if a line has a break in it *and* a sister line, the latter mends it, as it were, and the only effect of the break is a delicacy during the period over which the break extends. If the broken end of the line joins with the line of fortune, it is an indication that, at some time or other, the life has been in great danger, from which it has been protected by good luck.

Again, if the line appears to be short, an intense desire to live, supported by a strong phalanx of will and a good line of head, will often prolong it, the prolongation being marked on the hand by the appearance of sister lines or capillaries.

A line of life lying close to the thumb is a mark of sterility, especially if the lines of health and head are joined by a star.

An island on the line denotes an illness during the period of its length, generally caused by some excess shown elsewhere on the hand. If the line of health is absent, the island denotes biliousness and indigestion; an island at the very commencement of the line betrays some mystery of birth, some fatality, or some hereditary disease.

## The Line of Mars

In some hands we find inside the line of life, and running parallel and close to it, a second or sister line known in cheirosophy as the Line of Mars, or the Martial Line [vide Plate I.] Like all sister lines, it repairs and mitigates the effects of breaks in the main line; and it derives its name from the fact that it gives to soldiers great successes in arms, especially if it is clear and red in colour.

It gives, together with riches and prosperity, a great heat and violence to the passions, which with this line, if uncontrolled, are apt to become brutish. Its influence lasts throughout the period during which it follows the line of life; and De Peruchio says that there is always a love affair at the age at which it begins.

# The Line of Heart

This line should be neat, well coloured, and extending from the Mount of Jupiter to the outside of the hand under the Mount of Mercury, not broad and pale, or thick and red, but well traced, and of a good normal colour; such a condition of the line indicates a good heart, an affectionate disposition, with an equable temper and good health.

The strength of the affection is in proportion to the length of the line; if the line, instead of beginning at the Mount of Jupiter, begins upon the Mount of Saturn, the subject will be more sensual than Platonic in his affections.

Traced right across the hand, [from side to side,] it indicates an excess of affection which produces jealousy and suffering in consequence thereof, especially if the Mount of the Moon is high.

If it is chained in its formation, the subject is an inveterate flirt, and, unless the rest of the hand be very strong, will be much subject to palpitations of the heart.

Bright red in colour, the line denotes violence in affairs of the heart, and, on the other hand, a pale line, broad and chained, betrays a cold-blooded *roue,* if not a condition of heart utterly blasé. A lived or yellow colour betrays subjection to liver complaints.

The line should be close underneath, well up to the bases of the mounts; a line which lies close to that of the head throughout its length, betrays evil instincts, avarice, envy, hypocrisy, and duplicity.

A line of heart which begins quite suddenly without branches or rays beneath the Mount of Saturn, foreshadows a short life and a sudden death. If the line is very thin and runs right across the hand, it indicates cruelty even to murderous instincts.

If the line, instead of terminating on the Mounts of Jupiter or Saturn, seems to disappear between the first and second fingers, it betokens a long life of unremitting labour.

If to a large line of heart a subject add the Girdle of Venus and a high Mount of the Moon, he will be a victim to the most unreasoning jealousy.

If in a hand there be found no line of heart, it is an unfailing sign of treachery, hypocrisy, and the worst instincts, and, unless the line of health be very good, the subject will be liable to heart disease, and runs a grave danger of a sudden early death.

A line which is much broken up denotes inconstancy, and often these subjects are woman-haters. A single break shows a feebleness of the heart, and the cause of that feebleness may always be found in some excess or evil development of a mount-fatality shown by a development of the Mount of Saturn; foolishness shown by an equal development of the Mounts of Saturn and Apollo; pride shown by the Mount of Apollo; folly or avarice shown by the Mount of Mercury.

A quantity of little lines cutting across the line diagonally indicate many misfortunes of the heart, arising originally from weakness of the heart or liver.

## A Most Fortunate Sign

The line dividing at the end and going in three branches to the Mount of Jupiter, is a most fortunate sign, indicating riches and good luck. Any forking of the line which sends a branch on to the Mount of Jupiter is good; even if the branch goes in between the fingers of Jupiter and Saturn, this still indicates good fortune, but of a more quiet and undisturbing description. But a forking line which sends one ray upon the Mount of Jupiter and the other upon the Mount of Saturn, betrays errors and failures in the search after success, and fanaticism in religion.

If the line is quite bare under the finger of Jupiter at its commencement, there is great danger of poverty; a similar bareness at the percussion indicates sterility; a fork under Jupiter also gives the subject energy and enthusiasm in love. A line quite bare of branches throughout its length indicates dryness of heart and want of affection.

If the line touches the base of the finger of Jupiter, the subject will be unsuccessful in all his undertakings, unless the line of fortune be exceptionally good.

A mark like a deep scar across the line betrays a tendency to apoplexy; red spots or holes in the line denote wounds either physical or moral. White marks on the line denote conquests in love; a point on the line means grief of the heart, and, according to its position, you can tell by whom it was caused, thus:—Under the

Mount of Apollo the cause was an artist, or a celebrity—i.e., the grief is connected with art or ambition; under the Mount of Mercury the grief is caused by a man of science, a lawyer, or a doctor.

## Faculty for occultism

If the line curls round the first finger, it is a sign of a marvellous faculty for occultism and the possession of high occult powers.

Joined to the line of head under the Mounts of Jupiter or Saturn, is a sign of a great danger threatening the life, and of sudden and violent death, if the sign is repeated in both hands. If the line turns down on to the line of head, with a ray across it, as at h, in Plate V, it is a sign of a miserable marriage, or deep griefs of the heart.

A ray from the line to the Mount of Saturn, reaching to the base of the finger, [as at *m,* in Plate VI.], is a very bad sign in a woman's hand, immeasurably and even fatally increasing the dangers of maternity.

Lines from the quadrangle to the line of heart, [as at i.i.i, in Plate V.], denote aptitude for science, curiosity, research, and versatility, which often culminates in uselessness.

A curved line from the line of heart to the Mount of the Moon [stopping abruptly at the line of heart], [as at j, in Plate V], denotes murderous tendencies and instincts.

## The Line of Head

This line should be joined to the line of life at its immediate commencement, and leaving it directly should trace a strong ray across the hand to the top of the Mount of the Moon, clear and well coloured, without ramifications or forking, uninterrupted and regular; such a formation indicates good sense, clear judgment, cleverness, and strength of will.

Pale and broad, it indicates feebleness or want of intellect. Short—i.e., reaching only to the Plain of Mars,—it betrays weak ideas and weak will. [Stopping under the Mount of Saturn, it foreshadows an early sudden death]. Chained, it betrays a want of fixity of ideas and vacillation of mind. Long and very thin, it denotes treachery and infidelity. Of unequal thickness, twisted, and badly coloured, it betrays a feeble liver and want of spirit; such subjects are always avaricious.

# Multiplicity of Rays and Lines

A long line of head gives domination to a character—i.e., domination of self as opposed to the domination of others, which is indicated by a large thumb. A long line of head in a many-rayed and lined hand gives great self-control and coolness in danger and difficulties, and the strength of the head [shown by the long line] causes the subject to reason out and utilize the intuitive powers and instinctive promptings indicated by the multiplicity of rays and lines in the hand.

Very long and straight,—i.e., cutting the hand in a straight line from the line of life to the percussion,—it indicates an excess of reasoning habits, overcalculation, and over-economy, denoting avarice and meanness.

The excessive economy [avarice] of this line may be greatly modified by a softness of the hand or a high development of the Mounts of Jupiter or of Apollo.

If instead of joining the line of life at its commencement it only leaves it under the Mount of Saturn, it is a sure indication that the education has been acquired and the brain developed late in life; or, if the line of life is short, and the line of head also, it foreshadows a grave danger of sudden death. A like commencement, the line reaching across to the Mount of Mars, the line of heart being thin and small, indicates struggles and misfortunes arising from infirmities of temper or errors of calculation, unless the line of fortune is excep-tionally good. Such a subject will often appear benevolent, but his benevolence will generally be found to be only of a nature which gives pleasure to himself, and is usually more theoretical than practical.

The line must lie at a good regular distance from that of the heart; lying close up to it throughout its length, it betrays weakness and palpitations of the organ.

## Good Line of Head

Remember that an extremely good line of head may so influence the whole hand as to dominate other evil signs which may be found there, especially if the Mount of Mars be also high; such a combination gives to a subject energy, circums-pection, constancy, coolness, and a power of resistance, which goes a long way towards combating any evil or weak tendencies which may be found in his hand.

If the line stops abruptly under the Mount of Saturn it forewarns of a cessation of the intelligence, of [with other signs] death in early youth; stopping similarly under the finger of Apollo, it betrays inconstancy in the ideas and a want of order in the mind.

If, though visible, it appears joined to the line of life for some way before leaving it to go across the hand, it indicates timidity and want of confidence, which give dullness and apathy to the life, and which are overcome with difficulty. When this sign appears in an otherwise clever hand, the most strenuous efforts should be made to counteract this want of self-reliance, which is so serious an obstacle to success. Joined to the line of life in a really strong and clever hand, the indication will be of caution and circumspection.

Thin in the centre for a short space, the line indicates a nervous illness, neuralgia, or some kindred disease.

Separated from the line of life at its commen-cement and going well across the hand, it indicates intelligence, self-reliance, and spontaneity. With a long thumb it indicates, ambition. Separate from the line of life, and short or weak, it betrays carelessness, fantasy, jealousy, and deceit; often these subjects have bad sight. Separated thus, but connected by branches or ramifications, it indicates an evil temper and capriciousness; connected in a good hand there is danger in this sign of brusquerie, and a too great promptitude of decision, which often leads to error. With the Mounts of Saturn or Mars prominently developed, it is a sign of great audacity or imprudence, but it is a useful prognostic [within limits] for public characters or actors, giving them enthusiasm and boldness of manner in public, and the gift of eloquence by reason of their self-confidence. A *long* line thus separated will give want of tact and discrimination, and an impulsive manner of speech, which is often inconvenient, and sometimes wounds.

## Want of Instinct of Real Life

If the line, instead of going straight across the hand to the base of the Mount of Mars or to the top of the Mount of the Moon, traces an oblique course to a termination *on* the Mount of the Moon, it is a sign of idealism, and want of instinct of real life. If it comes very low upon the mount it leads to mysticism and folly, even culminating in madness if the line of health is cut by it in both hands. In an otherwise fairly strong hand this declension upon the Mount of the Moon gives poetry and a love of the mystic or occult sciences, superstition, and an inclination to spiritualism. Such a formation, if the Mount of the Moon is rayed, generally gives a talent for literature. The line of head coming low upon the Mount of the Moon to a star, as at *g*, in Plate VIII., with stars on the Mounts of Venus and Saturn, as at *h* and *i*. and a weak line of heart, are terribly certain signs of hereditary madness. This extreme obliquity of the line always indicates a danger of madness, and these concomitant signs prove it to be hereditary, and probably unavoidable.

Again, if instead of going across the hand it turns up towards one of the mounts, it will show that the thoughts are entirely taken up by the qualities belonging to the respective mounts; thus turning up to the Mount of Mercury commerce will be the prevailing instinct, and will bring good fortune; or, turning towards the Mount of Apollo, a desire for reputation will be the continual thought. If it points between the fingers of Apollo and Mercury, it signifies success in art brought by scientific treatment. If the line goes right up on to the mount it will denote a folly of the quality—thus, for instance, ending on Mercury it will denote occultism and deceit; on Apollo, the mania of art; and on Saturn, the mania of religion.

## A Prognostic of Early Death

Any turning up of the line of head towards that of the heart denotes a weak mind, which lets his heart and his passions domineer over his reason; if it *touches* the line of heart it is a prognostic of early death. If it cuts through the line of heart and ends upon the Mount of Saturn, if foreshadows death from a wound to the head. I have seen this sign verified in two terrible instances. If it turns up to the line of heart and confounds itself, which runs a great risk of terminating in madness.

Turning back towards the thumb. The line of head denotes intense egotism and misfortune in consequence thereof.

## Sure Sign of Good Fortune and Inheritances

A break in the line of head nearly always indicates an injury to the head. Broken under the finger of Saturn, and the broken ends overlapping, as at *a,* in Plate IX, the prognostic is especially certain, but in a bad hand it is said to be a sign of the scaffold, or, at any rate, of the loss of a member, even if the sign appears in one hand only. Much broken up it is a sign of headaches and general weakness of the head, resulting in loss of memory and want of continuity in the ideas. Such a breaking up will rob a long phalanx of will of much of its power, and long fingers of much of their spirit of minutiae. If with this shattered line of the head we find a cross in the Plain of Mars, the rays terminating in points or spots and short nails, it is a grave warning of a tendency to epilepsy.

Split throughout its length is a strengthening sign if other indications of madness appear in the hand, but if the line is distinctly *double* [*i.e.,* if it is accompanied by a sister line] it is a sure sign of good fortune and inheritances.

# Split and Sister Line

If the line is forked at the end, with one of the "prongs" descending upon the Mount of the Moon, [as at *b,* in Plate X,] we have a certain indication of lying, hypocrisy, and deceit. Such a man, even with a good hand, will be a clever sophist, never off his guard, ready at all times with [if necessary] an ingenious rearrangement of facts to suit the needs of the immediate present. This forking has somewhat the effect of short nails, giving to a subject a love of controversy and argument. If the rays or "prongs" of the fork are so long that one extends right across the hand, and the other comes well down to the rascette, it has the dual effect of a long line of head, and of a line of head which descends far upon the Mount of the Moon, giving at once poetry and realism—*i.e.,* a capability of making a practical use of poetic inspirations. A good line of Apollo gives *great* talent to a forked line of head, from its power of seeing all round a subject, and of considering it from all points. If one ray of the fork goes up to touch the line of the heart, and the other descends upon the Mount of the Moon, it betrays the sacrifice of all things to an affection, and if with this sign the line of Saturn or fortune stops short at the line of heart, it denotes that this infatuation has brought ruin with it. The two signs are nearly always concomitant.

Cut by a multitude of little lines, the line of head indicates a short life, with many illnesses and headaches. If the little cross lines are confined to the middle of the line of head it is a sign of dishonesty.

A cross in the middle of the line is a foresha-dowing of near approaching death. Or of a mortal wound if the line is also broken at this point.

Red points indicate wounds; white ones indicate discoveries in science or inventions. Black points, ailments according to the mount most developed in the hand. Thus with the Mount of Saturn, toothaches; with the Mount of Venus, deafness; with the Mount of Apollo, diseases of the eyes [especially if a star appear at the junction of the finger of Apollo and the palm]. These points are often connected with similar spots on the line of life by rays or lines, which enable us to pronounce with certainty the ages at which the subject has suffered from these maladies.

A knotting up of the line betrays an impulse to murder, which, if the knot is pale, is past, but which, if the knot is deep red, is to come.

Capilalry lines [vide fig. 9, Plate II.] on the line of head are a sign of a well-ordered mind and a good disposition.

An island in the line of head is an indication of acutely sensitive nerves.

A star upon the line is generally a sign of a very bad wound, bringing danger of folly with it.

## Sign of Disappointment in Love

If a line be found connecting a star on the Mount of Venus with a spot on the line of head, [as at c c, in Plate IX,] it indicates a deeply-rooted and ever-remembered disappointment in love.

If a line extend from the line of head to the root of the finger of Jupiter, [as at I, in Plate VII,] it indicates intense pride and vanity which is easily wounded; if it ends at a star upon the finger, [as at j, in Plate VIII,] it is a sign of extreme good luck; but if it ends at the same place with a cross, the luck will be, on the contrary, extremely bad. This little line, joined by the line of Saturn or fortune, vanity, reaching even to folly.

## The Line of Saturn, or Fortune

The line of Saturn, or fortune, has three principal points of departure for its base: it may start from the line of life, as at d, in Plate IX; from the *rascette,* as at *e;* or from the Mount of the Moon, as at f. Starting from the line of life, the line of fortune indicates that the luck in life is the result of one's own personal merit. If it starts from the wrist, or rascette, the fortune will be very good, especially if it traces a fine strong furrow on the Mount of Saturn; in the same direction, but commencing higher up from a point in the Plain of Mars, we get an indication of a painful, troubled life, especially if the line penetrates [as it often does] into the finger. If the line starts from the Mount of the Moon, it shows [if it goes straight to the Mount of Saturn] that the fortune is, to a great extent, derived from the caprice of the opposite sex. If from the Mount of the Moon the line goes to that of the heart, and, confounding itself therein, goes on up to the Mount of Jupiter, it is an infallible sign of a rich and fortunate marriage. You must guard against confounding a chance line from the Mount of the Moon to the line of Saturn with the line of Saturn starting from that Mount. If [besides the line of Saturn, as at e, in Plate IX] we have another line starting as at f, in Plate IX, and cutting instead of joining the line of Saturn, it betrays the fatal effects of imagination, culminating possibly in weakness, or evil to the mental capacity. Starting from the very base of the Mount of the Moon, and ending on the Mount of Saturn is an indication of prediction and clairvoyance.

Instead of going to the Mount of Saturn, the line may go up to some other mount, in which case it will have special significance; thus, going to the Mount of Mercury, we get fortune in commerce, eloquence, and science; going to the Mount of Apollo, we get fortune from art or wealth; going to the Mount of Jupiter, we find satisfied pride, and the attainment of the objects of our ambition.

## Indication of very Great Fortune

If the line, instead of stopping on the mount, goes right up to the second joint of the finger, we have the indication of very great frotune, which will be either very good or very bad according to the concomitant signs. Thus, with a good hand, this is a first-rate sign; but with a deep red line on the mount, and a star on the first phalanx of the finger, we have the indication of the worst possible fortune, ending in a violent death, probably on the scaflold. The line should just extend from the top of the rascette to the centre of the Mount of Saturn; reaching to the joint of the finger and palm, or penetrating into the rascette is a bad sign, being a sure indication of misery Starting from the rascette, and stopped at the line of heart, indicates a misfortune arising from a disappointment in love; or, in a weak hand, heart-disease. Similarly stopped at the line of head, the misfortune will arise from an error of calculation, of from an illness of the head.

If it only starts from the line of head it denotes labour, pain, and ill-health, unless the line of head is very good, when it will be an indication of fortune acquired late in life by the intelligence of the subject. Shorter still,—i.e., from the quadrangle to the Mount of Saturn,—the indications are still more unfortunate, being of great sorrows, and even of imprisonment. The evil prognostications of a line which goes into the third Phalanx of the finger of Saturn may be averted by the presence of a square on the mount.

If the line is stopped in the quadrangle, and then starts again at the line of heart, ending its course upon the mount, it denotes that though the luck will be obstructed and retarded, it will not be permanently spoilt, and the position in life will not be lost; and this is especially certain if a good line of Apollo is found in the hand.

## Age on the Line of Fate

And this brings us to the indications of age on the line of Saturn. The line starts from its base, and on it [as in Plate IV] one can tell by its breaks, and so on, approximately the ages at which events have occurred in a life: it must, however, be premised that these indications are not anything like as sure as those of the line of life. From the base of the line to the line of head we have thirty years, from the line of head to that of the heart we find the events of the life between thirty and fortyfive years, and thence to the top of the line takes us to the end of the life. Thus, for instance, if you see a gap, or break, in the line from the line of head to just below the line of heart, you can predict misfortunes between the ages of thirty and forty; and a connecting line will generally indicate the nature and cause of the ill-luck. Also it will often be found that in the right hand a misfortune will be marked on the line of Saturn, the exact date of which will be marked by a point on the line in the left hand.

The indications found upon the line of Saturn often explain and elucidate indications only dimly or vaguely traced upon the line of life, or in the rest of the hand.

## What the Line of Saturn Indicates?

A perfectly straight line, with branches going upwards from its two sides, indicates a gradual progress from poverty to riches. Twisted at the base, and straight at the top, it indicates early misfortunes, followed by good luck. Straightness, and good colour, from the line of heart upwards, always betokens good fortune in old age, with invention in science, and a talent for such pursuits as horticulture, agriculture, construction, and architecture. Split and twisted, the line of Saturn indicates ill-health from an abuse of pleasure. A twisted condition of the line always denotes quarrels, and a very good and well-traced line of Saturn will annul the evil indications of a badly formed line of life.

## Inconstancy of Fortune

A broken-up and ragged condition of the line betrays an inconstancy and changeability of fortune. Breaks in the line in the Plain of Mars, denote physical and moral struggles. Even, however, if it is broken up, it may be replaced by a very good development of the Mount of Saturn, or a favourable aspect of the Mount of Mars; and to the worst luck a high Mount of the Moon will give a calm and resignation, which rob it of much of its evil indication. A strong, irregular line of fortune, in a much-rayed and lined hand, betrays a constant irritability, and a super-sensitive condition of mind. A well-traced line of Saturn always gives a long life; broken up at the base is an indication of misery in early life; broken up at the base is an indication of misery in early life, up to the age at which the breaking up ceases. If it ends in a star on the mount, it foreshadows great misfortune, following great good luck; in a good hand this sign generally means that the misfortune is caused by the fault of others, *generally* of one's relations. For the line of Saturn to be lucky, there must be explanatory points in the hand for the luck to come from, and to find these is one of the most important tasks of the cheirosophist.

Cut by a multitude of little lines on the mount, we can safely foretell misfortunes late in life, after a long period of good luck. Cut by a line parting from the Mount of Venus, it denotes conjugal misery, or misfortune caused by a woman [g g, in Plate IX].

If the line is simply absent from a hand, it denotes an insignificant life, which takes things as they come, meeting with neither particularly good nor particularly bad fortune.

Forked, with one ray going to the Mount of Venus and the other to the Mount of the Moon, [as at n n, in Plate VI,] we find a strife for success, directed by the wildest imagination, and spurred on by love. If the line go well up, as in Plate VI, the ambition will be successful, after much struggle; but if the main line is broken or malformed, the necessary intrigues and caprices caused by the formation of the line will result in inevitable misfortune.

## Cross upon the Line

Any cross upon the line indicates a change of position or of prospects in life at the age indicated by the position of the cross upon the line [as in Plate IV]. in the very centre of the line it is always a misfortune, and the cause of it may nearly always be found upon the lines of head or life, showing the misfortune to arise from error or miscalculation, or from illnesses or the loss of friends.

A star at the base of the line [as at j, in Plate VII] denotes a loss of fortune, brought by the parents of the subject in early youth; if there be also a star on the Mount of Venus, [as at *h,* in Plate VIII,] the immediate cause is the early death of a parent.

An island on the line betrays, almost invariably, a conjugal infidelity; a star accompanying the island betokens a great misfortune arising therefrom. At the very

# Plate VIII

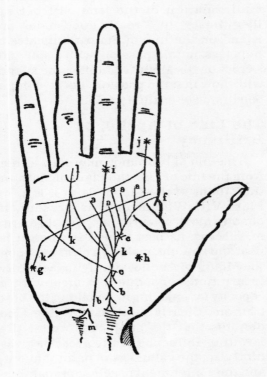

**Modifications of the Principal Lines**

base of a line, an island indicates a mystery connected with the birth of the subject, and with this sign, an extreme malformation of the line will betray illegitimacy. In a really good hand, an island on the line of Saturn indicates a hopeless, untold passion; with a star and a cross on the Mount of Jupiter, the island will show that the passion has been for a celebrated or exalted person.

## The Line of Apollo, or Brilliancy

The line of brilliancy may start either from the line of Life, the Plain of Mars, or the Mount of the Moon, as at k k k, in Plate VIII Whenever it is present, it denotes glory, celebrity, art, wealth, merit, or success; its best aspect is when it is neat and straight, making a clear cut upon the Mount of Apollo, signifying celebrity in art, and consequent riches, with a capacity for enjoying and making the best of them. Clearly marked, the line also denotes that the subject is under the favour or influence of the great; it gives him, also, the calmness of natural talent, and the contentment of self-approbation.

It is necessary that this line exist in a really lucky hand to make its good fortune absolute; a good Line of Saturn will be seriously compromised by the absence of this line.

With the Mounts of Jupiter and Mercury developed, this line is a certain indication of wealth, and such a subject will become celebrated by his fortune, dignity, and merit, no less than by his talents and scientific capacities.

## Very Bad Signs

Twisted fingers, or a hollow palm, are very bad signs with this line; for they show that the influences of the line are guided in an evil direction, and that the talents indicated by it are used for the attainment of bad ends.

With a long line of head, and a long finger of Apollo, the tendencies of the line will be material, the ambition and talents being turned towards the attainment of riches.

The line, to have all its highest artistic significations, should be well coloured; pale, it denotes that the subject is not actively artistic, but has merely the instincts of art, loving things that are brilliant and beautiful. In these respects

# Plate IX

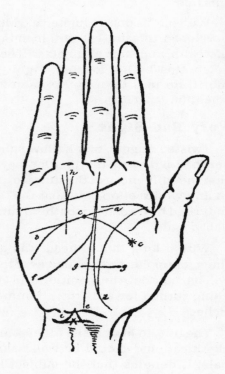

## Modifications of the Principal Lines

the indications are the same as those of a high Mount of Apollo *without* the line; such a formation also gives a love of the beautiful *without* production, the mount giving the instincts, and the line giving the talents, of art.

Absence of the line from a hand indicates want of success in projects and undertakings which would [if successful] lead to glory and success.

Much broken up it indicates a Jack-of-all-trades and an eccentricity in art which renders it of little avail to the owner.

Many little lines upon the mount point generally to an excess of artistic instinct, which generally falls by its own weight, and comes to nothing; it is much better to have only one line on the mount, unless all are equally clear and well traced. With two or three lines, a subject will often follow two or three different branches of art, without succeeding particularly in any one.

## Signs in the Quadrangle

If the line is confused and split up in the quadrangle, but clear above, we find misfortunes, having, however, good terminations. Any sign upon the line of Apollo in the quadrangle must be carefully observed, for they always denote worries, and are generally connected by a worry-line with the line of life and Mount of Venus, showing the times at which they occurred.

If the line is equally divided on the mount, as at *k*, in Plate VII, we find an equal balancing of two instincts, which ends in a nullity in the matter of art. Divided into a curved trident, as at *l*, in Plate IX, it is a sure indication of cast unrealized desires of wealth; if, however, the line divides into a pointed trident from the line of heart, as at h, in Plate X., we can safely announce future glory, riches, and celebrity arising from the personal merit; and if, instead of being joined at the heart, the three lines rise parallel and identical, as at *k*, in Plate V, tracing three fine troughs on the mount, we have these same indications intensified and made yet more certain.

## Obstacles to Artistic Success

Cross-lines on the mount are obstacles which stand in the way of artistic success, very often arising from the envy and malignity of others.

Cut by a line coming from the Mount of Saturn, as at *a,* in Plate X, poverty will stand in the way of complete success. Similarly cut by a line coming from the Mount of Mercury, as at *b,* in Plate X, the success and good fortune will be marred and prevented by inconstancy and changeableness of spirit.

A star on the mount is a good sign, indicating success and good luck, arising from the favour of others and the help of friends.

A cross upon the mount close to the line, or even touching it, denotes instinct of religion and piety.

A black spot at the junction of the lines of heart and of Apollo betrays a great danger, if not an imminent peril of blindness.

## The Line of Liver, or Health

The position which the liver line [line of health, or Lignea hepatica] occupies in the hand may be seen by looking at the Map of the hand, Plate I., but it will strike the cheirosophist, after very little experience, that this line fully developed in a hand is comparatively scarce, and the reason of this I take to be the comparatively unhealthy lives which the majority of people live nowadays. I have seen this line in a fresh young hand, beautifully traced and as clear as any of the others, and watching the hand have seen the line break up and practically disappear in the course of a few years.

## A powerful agent in prolonging Life

Long, clearly traced, and well coloured and proportioned, the line denotes good health, gaiety, a clear conscience, and success in life. If it is lengthened up to the upper part of the palm it is a sign that the good health of the subject will last well into old age. A thoroughly good line of health will counteract the evil effects of a poor line of life, being an indication of good digestion, which will always prove a powerful agent in prolonging life.

The line should not be joined to that of the life at its base, but just separated, as at d, in Plate X this will indicate long life; joined at this point with the line of life, it is a sure indication of weakness of the heart.

This line completely absent from a hand will render the subject vivacious in conversation, agile and quick in manner.

If the line is thick and blunt, it is a sign of sickness in old age; if it is very straight and thin, it is a sign of rigidity of spirit and manner. Red at the upper end, it betrays a tendency to headaches; thin and red in the centre, it is a sign of fever; red at the lower end is a sign of a weak heart; thus it will be seen that any unevenness of colour in this line is bad. Very red throughout its length indicates brutality and pride. A twisted and wavy liver line is a sign of biliousness, and very often of dishonesty, of which it is, at any rate, a strong confirmatory indication. Much broken or cut into, the line will betray a weak digestion.

Forked at the top so as to make a triangle with the line of head, [as at c, in Plate X,] it gives a great love of honours and power combined, always with a marvellous aptitude and capacity for occult sciences.

A coming sickness marks itself on this line by a little deep cross-line; a past sickness marks only the life or head lines, leaving merely a gap in the line of health.

The line of health making a good clear triangle with the lines of head and of fortune, we find a subject very clever at natural magic, Electro-biology, and the like, a great student of nature and of natural phenomena, with a high faculty of tuition, sometimes accompanied by second sight.

The line traced across upon the Mount of the Moon is a sure sign of caprice and of change in the course of the life of the subject.

A Long Island at the base of the line denotes a somnambulist.

A sister line to this liver line indicates strong and unprincipled avarice.

## The Cephalic line, or Via Lasciva

This line is rare; it is often confounded with the line of health, and is still more often regarded as a sister line to the liver line, but it is quite a separate line from itself, appearing only *conjointly with* the line of head, though it diverges considerably from it in the manner shown in the map of the Hand.

It generally betokens cunning, and often faithlessness, especially if twisted, though these indications are considerably modified the more distinct it be from the line of health. It gives ardour and fervour to the passions, and reaching up to the Mount of Mercury, it indicates constant good luck arising from eloquence and pure talent.

Stars on the line generally betoken riches, but often they betray serious troubles and struggles in front of, and accompanying them. Joined by a ray to the Line of Apollo, the line is a sure indication of wealth.

It used to be customary to look upon this line [as its ancient name denotes] as a sign of lasciviousness, but this indication only belongs to it if it runs across into the Mount of Venus.

## The Girdle of Venus

This line, fortunately not universal, may be taken, as whole, to be a *bad* sign in any hand, indicating a tendency to deauchery, which it is extremely difficult to conquer.

To a good hand, however, this line will expend itself by giving energy and ardour in every undertaking entered into by the subject, and this favourable influence of the line is the more certain if it is clear, neat, and going off upon the Mount of Mercury, [as at *l l,* Plate VII]. To a good hand this will give merely love of pleasure and energy therein.

It generally makes a subject hysterical and nervous, with a great tendency towards spiritualism and sorcery, accompanied by a more or less chronic state of melancholy and depression. There is also very frequently a talent for and a love of literature, and lyric poetry.

If the lines of fortune or of Apollo are cut by the Girdle of Venus, so as apparently to shatter them in two at this point on the mount, it is a sign of obstacles to the success and misfortunes, probably the result of excessive passion, or ardour in the pursuit of pleasure.

Coming up on to the Mount of Mercury, as at *l,* in Plate V, the subject will add to all the other evil indication of the line the vices of lying and theft.

Cut upon the Mount of Apollo by a short deep line, [as at *o,* in Plate VI,] it is a sign of loss of fortune, caused by dissipation and debauchery.

Crossed by a quantity of little lines, it is a sure sign of a hysterical nature, especially if the Mount of Venus, or of the Moon, or both, are highly developed.

We have now considered the principal lines, and discussed them with considerable minuteness; a careful retrospect will show the reader that the indications of the lines are easily found by examining their condition with reference to the mounts and the other lines of the palm. Each mount or line having its peculiar significations and effects, and bringing them to bear upon the *other* mounts and lines and the qualities indicated by them, by juxtaposition or connection with them by means of lines, rays, or signs.

Often, however, we find lines in a hand, which cannot be accounted for by any of the foregoing rules, and these [which are called "chance lines"] are made the special subject of a future chapter. the signs found in the palm, though they have already frequently been refered to, will be our next consideration, with reference to their special and individual significance.

# CHAPTER FOUR

## The Signs in the Plam

G reat attention must be paid to the signs which are found very frequently upon, or close to, the mounts and lines of the hands, for they very greatly modify and alter the recognized significance of the mounts or lines, and generally carry with them an indication entirely their own.

## The Star

A Star, [fig. 10, Plate XI] whenever it appears, is generally the indication of some event we cannot possibly control; it is generally a danger, and always something unavoidable. Whether, however, it is good or bad, depends of course upon the aspect of the lines, particularly of the line of fortune. This, however, is fixed—that a star whenever it is found, always means something, and what that something is,

# Plate XI

Fig. 10.
The Star

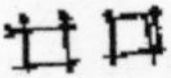

Fig. 11.
The Square

Fig. 12.
The Spot

Fig. 13.
The Circle

Fig. 17.
The Grille

Fig. 14.
The Island

Fig. 15.
The Triangle

Fig. 16.
The Cross

## Signs Found in the Hand

be it the task of the cheirosophist to discover.

On the Mount of Jupiter it signifies gratified ambition, good luck, honour, love, and success, With a cross on this mount it indicates a happy marriage with some one of brilliant antecedents or high position.

On the Mount of Saturn it indicates a great fatality, generally a very bad one, indicating, with corroborative signs, probable murder, and in a criminal or otherwise very bad hand a probability of death upon the scaffold.

On the Mount of Apollo, with no line of Apollo in the hand, it betokens wealth without happiness, and celebrity after a hazardous struggle for it. With the line of brilliancy it denotes excessive celebrity, as the combined result of labour and talent; with several lines also on the mount it is a sure indication of wealth.

On the Mount of Mercury it betrays dishonesty and theft. On the Mount of Mars violence leading to homicide.

On the Mount of the Moon it indicates hypocrisy and dissimulation, with misfortune resulting from excess of the imagination. The old cheiromants looked upon this as a warning of death by drowning, and stated that combined with a high mount invaded by the line of head, it indicated suicide by drowning.

On the base of the Mount of Venus it indicates a misfortune brought about by the influence of women.

## On the Phalanges of the Fingers

On the first [outer] phalanx of any finger but [especially of that of Saturn] a star indicates either strange good luck or else folly. On the third [or lowest] phalanx of the finger of Saturn, a star warns the subject of a danger of assassination, and if at this point it is joined by the line of Saturn, a disgraceful death is almost inevitable, resulting, as a rule, from the vices shown elsewhere in the hand.

On the base of the phalanx of logic of the thumb,—in fact, on the junction of the phalanx of logic and the Mount of Venus,— it points to a misfortune connected with a woman, probably indicating an unhappy marriage, which will be the curse of the subject's whole existence, unless the Mount of Jupiter be developed, in which case there is a probability that the subject will get over it.

A star on a voyage line indicates with certainty death by drowning.

If a star be found in the centre of the quadrangle, the subject, though true and honest as the day, will be the absolute plaything of women, a trait which will result in a misfortune, from which, however, he will recover in time.

Thus it will be seen that a star is almost the most important sign to seek for in a hand.

## The Square

The appearance of a square [fig. 11, Plate XI] on the hand always denotes power or energy of the qualities indicated by the mount or line on which it is found. It is a sign of good sense, and of cold, unimpassioned justice.

It may either appear as a neat quadrangular figure, traced as if with a punch, or it may be formed of the [apparently] accidental crossing of principal and chance lines. It will often appear enclosing a bad sign, from the effects of which it entirely protects the subject.

Wherever it is found it always denotes protection; thus round a break in the line of life it betokens recovery from that illness; or on the line of Saturn, it will protect the subject from the evil effects of a badly-formed line, or of bad signs found thereon.

A star on the Mount of Saturn surrounded by a square denotes an escape from assassination; a square with red points at the corners denotes a preservation from fire.

The square has one evil significance— that is, when it is on the Mount of Venus, close to the line of life; under these circumstances it is a warning of imprisonment of some sort or another.

## The spot

A spot, [figs. I and 12,] wherever found and of whatever colour, always denotes a malady; placed upon a line, it is nearly always the mark of wound; on the line of head it denotes a blow to the head, and consequent folly.

A white spot on the line of heart denotes a conquest in love; a white spot on the line of head points to a scientific discovery. A red spot is the sign of a wound; a black or blue spot is the sign of a disease, generally of a nervous character. The white spot is the only comparatively harmless one.

## The Circle

The circle [fig. 13, Plate IX] is a comparatively rare sign. which has only one good significance—that is, when it appears on the Mount of Apollo, where it indicates glory and success.

On the mount of the Moon it denotes danger of death by drowning; on any other mount it gives a dangerous brilliancy.

On any line it is bad, denoting always an injury to the organ or quality represented. Thus, on the line of heart, it betrays weakness of the heart, and on the line of head it forewarns a subject of blindness.

## The Island

The island [fig. 14] should perhaps more properly have been noticed in treating of the lines generally; but it is a sign so distinct from any ordinary formation of the line, that I have thought it best to consider it in this place as a sign proper.

An island means always one of two things; either it is the mark of something disgraceful, or else it betrays a hereditary evil. It is the more often a hereditary malady of the line, as, for instance, on the line of head it will show a hereditary weakness of the head, or on the line of heart it betrays a hereditary heart disease, and so on.

As for the disgraceful indications of the island, it should be taken to mean more properly that the chance, *i.e.,* the temptation, will occur; but a long line of head and a strong phalanx of will on the thumb will always annul the most evilly-disposed island.

On the line of heart it means in a good hand heart disease, or, in a bad one, adultery.

On the head line of , if it occurs on the Plain of Mars, it shows a murderous tendency; if beyond the Plain of Mars, it betrays evil thoughts. On a good hand it will merely indicate hereditary head weakness.

On the line of liver or health it betrays a tendency to theft or dishonesty; in a good hand a weak digestion, or an intestinal complaint.

On the line of life an island indicates some mystery connected with the birth of the subject.

## The Triangle

The triangle [fig. 15] always denotes an aptitude for science, and may be formed either neatly and by itself, or by the [apparently] chance coincidence of three lines.

On the Mount of Jupiter it indicates diplomatic ability. On the Mount of Saturn it betrays aptitude for occult sciences and necromancy, a sign which becomes very sinister and evil if there be also a star on the third phalanx of this finger. On the Mount of Apollo a triangle indicates science in art; on the Mount of Mercury, talent in politics; on the Mount of Mars, science in war; on the Mount of the Moon, wisdom in mysticism; and on the Mount of Venus, calculation and interest in love.

## The Cross

The cross [fig. 16) is seldom a favourable sign, unless it is very clear and well marked, when by accentuating the qualities of the mount or line, it may have a good significance. It nearly always indicates a change of position.

Its one undoubtedly good significance is when it appears on the Mount of Jupiter, where it denotes a happy marriage, especially if the lines of Saturn or of Apollo start from the Mount of the Moon.

On the Mount of Saturn it denotes error and fanaticism in religion or occult science, leading to the more evil forms of mysticism.

On the Mount of Apollo it betrays errors of judgment in art, unless there be also a fine line of Apollo, which will give to the cross the significance of wealth.

On the Mount of Mercury it indicates dishonesty, and even theft.

On the Mount of Mars it denotes danger arising from quarrelsomeness and obstinacy.

A cross on the mount of Moon will indicate a liar, and a man who deceives even himself if it is large; but if it is small, it will merely indicate reverie and mysticism.

## What Denotes Fatal Love?

On the Mount of Venus it denotes a single and a fatal love, unless another cross appear on the Mount of Jupiter to render the union happy.

At the bottom of the hand, near the line of life,—i.e., in the lower angle of the triangle,—a cross denotes a struggle, ending in a change of position in life, which is the more radical according as the cross is more or less clearly marked at this point.

## The "Croix Mystique"

This is a sign so entirely by itself that I devote a separate discussion to it. It is found traced with more or less distinctness in the quadrangle beneath the finger of Saturn.

It always gives to a subject mysticism, superstition, and occultism, or, with a very good hand, religion. If it is very large it betrays exaggerated superstition, bigotry, and hallucination.

If it is clearly traced in both hands, it betrays folly arising from the excessive influence of the principal mount; thus, with Jupiter developed, over-ambition; with Saturn, misanthropy; with Apollo, extreme vanity or miserliness; and with Venus erotomania.

If the "Croix Mystique" is joined to the line of Saturn, it foretells good fortune arising from religion.

If it is displaced, so as to lie, as it were, between the Mounts of Mars and of the Moon, [as at p, in Plate VI,] it indicates a changeability of disposition, which will head to good fortune.

## The Grille

The grille [fig. 17] is generally the indication of obstacles, and of the faults of a mount whereon it is found. But if there be no mount particularly elevated in the hand, it will so emphasize a mount, if it is found upon one, as to make *it* the principal mount and keynote of the interpretation of the hand.

On the Mount of Jupiter it indicates superstition, egoism, pride, and the spirit of domination.

On the Mount of Saturn it foretells misfortune and want of luck.

On the Mount of Apollo it betrays folly and vanity, and a great desire of glory, joined to impotence and error.

On the Mount of Mercury it tells of a serious tendency towards theft, cunning, and dishonesty.

On the Mount of Mars it forewarns a violent death, or, at any rate, some great danger thereof.

A grille on the Mount of the Moon indicates sadness, restlessness, discontent, and a morbid imagination.

If on a hand which is much covered with lines it shows a constant movement and state of excitement. If there be a star on the Mount of Saturn this sign tells of the wildest exaltation, nervous spasms, and continual anxieties and disquietude.

With a well-traced line of Apollo and a grille on the Mount of the Moon we find poetry, and great talent for lyrics and literature.

The grille on the Mount of Venus is often a bad sign, denoting lasciviousness and morbid curiosity, especially with the Girdle of Venus traced in the hand. With a strong phalanx of will and a long line of head and the line of Apollo, or brilliancy, this sign merely results in a nervous excitement, which is in no way pernicious or evil in its effects, giving a refinement and daintiness to the passions.

A strong phalanx of will, with a good line of head and of Apollo, will *always* greatly modify the sinister effects of the grille, excepting when it is found on the Mounts of Jupiter or Saturn, when it is practically irremediable.

## The Signs of the Planets

Besides the above comparatively ordinary signs we find in some instances [though such instances are excessively rare] the actual sign of a planet actually traced on a mount. As a rule, when this occurs the rest of the hand is perfectly plain, the whole force of the character being concentrated in the quality indicated by the "precipitation" of the planetary sign. As these are so intensely rare, I will give examples only which I have had the fortune actually to see myself.

The sign of Mercury traced upon the Mount of Jupiter gives great administrative talent and noble eloquence. The sign of the Moon on the Mount of Jupiter leads to intense mysticism and error. The sign of Mercury on the Mount of Apollo gives great celebrity and eloquence in science.

A mount sometimes also, instead of being high or rayed, has its own sign traced upon it; thus on Jupiter, on Saturn, on Apollo, on Mercury, on Mars, on the Moon, and on Venus. These signs, of course, intensify the qualities of the mounts to an extremely marked and extraordinary extent.

## The Signs upon the fingers

We have dealt above only with the signs found upon the palm of the hand. We have also to consider the lines and signs which find themselves traced upon the fingers, which signs have also their special significations.

Lines on the first phalanx of a finger always denote a weakness or failing of the quality of the finger. If the lines are twisted and confused they foreshadow danger to the subject from the qualities of the finger. A single deep ray on the first phalanx of a finger indicates an idealism or folly connected with the quality.

Lines from the first into the second phalanges unite, as it were, the worlds of idealism and reason, causing the subject to mix a certain amount of reason with all the promptings of his imagination. In the same way lines connecting the second and third phalanges unite reason and matter, and the subject will always set about his worldly affairs in a reasonable and sensible manner.

One short line, sharply traced on each phalanx of each finger gives energy and ardour to the qualities of the finger; cross lines, however, are obstacles in the way of the proper development of the characteristics of the finger.

## Signs on the First Finger, or Index

A line extending from the mount, through the third phalanx into the second, gives a character in which reason and thought is mingled with audacity.

Cross lines on the third phalanx indicate inheritances according to the older cheirosophists; on the second phalanx they denote general debility, and if they extend all the way from one side of the nail round the ball of the finger to the other side, they foreshadow wounds to the head.

A pair of crosses on the second phalanx are a sign of the friendship of great men.

A star on the first phalanx indicates great good fortune; a star on the second phalanx indicates mischief and boldness, unless it is connected with the first phalanx by a line, in which case it becomes a sign of modesty. A star on the third phalanx is a sign of unchastity.

A crescent upon the first phalanx is a sure sign of imprudence, which may bring about very grave results.

## Signs on the Second or Middle Finger

A line from the Mount of Saturn across the third phalanx of the finger indicates prosperity in arms; if it is oblique it foretells death in battle.

Many lines just penetrating into the mount denote cruelty; if they go the whole length of the finger they indicate melancholy; or, if they are very parallel and equal, they denote success in mining operations. If the lines are confined to the first phalanx they denote avarice. Twisted lines on the third phalanx denote ill luck.

A triangle on the third phalanx indicates mischief and ill luck.

A star on the first phalanx indicates great misfortune, and if it is on the *side* of the finger it betrays a probability of death, which will, however, be in a just cause.

## Signs on the Third, or Ring Finger

A single line running the entire length of the finger is a sure indication of great renown. Many lines are a sign of losses, probably occasioned by women.

Straight lines on the third phalanx indicate prudence and happiness. Turning to one side of the finger they indicate great success, but not success accompanied by wealth. If the lines on the third phalanx penetrate on to the mount they indicate good fortune, accompanied by loquacity and often by arrogance.

A line extending from the third phalanx into the second is a sign of goodness and cleverness, accompanied by good fortune. Cross lines placed upon this phalanx indicate difficulties in the way, which will have to be surmounted.

A crescent on the third phalanx signifies unhappiness, and a cross at the same place signifies extravagance.

## Signs on the Fourth or Little Finger

A line throughout the length of this finger signifies success in science and uprightness of mind; three lines similarly running right down the finger are a sign of research in chimaerical and impossible sciences.

Deep lines on the first phalanx denote weakness of constitution; a cross on the same place is significant of poverty and consequent celibacy.

Lines on the second phalanx are an indication of research in occult sciences. If they are confused and coarse they betray unchastity.

A line from the third into the second phalanx indicates eloquence and consequent success. If the line is twisted it gives great sharpness and cunning in defence of self. If this line starts from the mount it is a still surer sign of prosperity and success.

One thick line, a scar, on the third phalanx, betrays a tendency to theft. A star on the same phalanx denotes eloquence.

A line extending from the mount into the third phalanx is significant of great intelligence and astuteness.

## Signs on the Thumb

Signs are much rarer upon the thumb than upon fingers, but still they are sometimes found.

A subject who has several lines traced along the entire length of the phalanx of will, will make a faithful lover, having the gift of constancy and fidelity.

Cross lines upon the thumb denote riches.

Lines extending from the mount onto the phalanx of logic, are a sure sign that the subject is much beloved.

A star on the phalanx of logic in a female hand is a sign of great riches.

A ring right round the joint which separates the phalanges of will and logic was held by the older cheiromants to be the sign of the scaffold.

## THE TRIANGLE, QUADRANGLE, AND THE RASCETTE

### The Triangle

The triangle [called also the Triangle of Mars, from the fact that it is filled by the Plain of Mars] is the name given to the triangular space enclosed between the lines of life, head, and health. When [as is often the case,] the line of health is not present in a hand, or so very badly traced as to be almost invisible, its place must be supplied by an imaginary line drawn from the base of the line of life to the end of the

line of head, *or,* this side of the triangle
may be formed of the line of Apollo.

Though it must be considered as a
whole, still each part of the triangle has
its special signification; thus, it is
composed of the *upper angle* formed by
the junction of the lines of life and head;
the *inner angle* formed by the junction of
the lines of head and health; and the *lower
angle*, formed by the junction of the line
of health and life. [The lower angle may
also be formed of the junction of the lines
of health and of fortune.]

If the triangle is well traced and neat,
being composed of good even lines, [as in
Plate X] it indicates good health, good luck,
a long life, and courageous disposition.

If it is large it denotes audacity,
liberality of mind, genrosity, and nobleness
of soul; to have these significations it must
be well and healthfully coloured, not livid,
or approaching to deep red.

If it is small and formed of lines curving
much inwards it betrays pettiness,
cowardice, and avarice.

Sometimes a triangle will form itself in
a hand which began by being absolutely
without it; this is a sign that the health,

originally bad, has improved with advancing years.

If the skin inside the triangle is rough and hard, it is an indication of hardihood and strength of nerve.

## What Betokens continual Bad Luck?

A cross in the triangle denotes an extremely quarrelsome and contrary disposition. It betrays a state of mind best described by the American expression "cussedness." Many crosses in the triangle foretell continual bad luck.

A crescent in the triangle, as at *f,* in Plate X, betrays an extremely capricious disposition, often indicating brutality and a love of bullying. If it is joined to the line of head, as at g, in the same figure, it is a prognostic of a violent death brought upon oneself by an imprudence or a want of calculation. Joined, however, similarly to the line of health, as at *h,* it is a sign of power and of success accompanied by excellent health.

A star in the triangle denotes riches, but riches obtained with much difficulty and worry. If the star is the termination of a worry line it indicates a sorrow, and if the worry line comes from a star in the Mount of Venus, it denotes that the sorrow has resulted from the death of a parent or of some near relation.

## The Upper Angle

The upper angle [I, in Plate X] should be neat, clearly traced, and well pointed; it indicates refinement and delicacy of mind.

Blunt and short, it betrays a heavy, dull intellect, and a want of delicacy. *Very blunt,*—i.e., placed under the Mount of Saturn,—it betrays a great danger of misery, and a tendency to avarice.

The other extreme, however,—i.e., very pointed,—is a sign of malignity, envy, and finesse.

## The Inner Angle

The inner angle, [k, in Plate X,] if clear and well marked, indicates long life and a quick intelligence.

Very sharp, it betrays a highly nervous temperament, and nearly always a mischievous disposition.

Obtuse and confused, this angle denotes heaviness of intelligence, dullness of instinct, and, as a result consequence, obstinacy and inconstancy.

## The Lower Angle

The Lower angle, [l, in Plate X,] well defined, and just open, [as at d,] gives strong indications of good health and a good heart. If it is too sharp—in fact, if it is closed up—it denotes avarice and debility. If it is heavy and coarse, composed of many rays, or of a confusion of lines, it betrays a bad nature, with a strong tendency to rudeness and laziness.

Thus it will be seen that it is most important to observe, with reference to its component lines, the formation of the triangle and of its constituent angles.

## The Quadrangle

The quadrangle [vide Map, Plate I.] is the square space contained between the lines of heart and of head. It may be said to be bounded at its two ends by imaginary lines, drawn perpendicularly to the line of head from the crevice between the first and second fingers, and from the crevice between the third and fourth fingers.

It should be fairly large and wide at the two ends, [but not too narrow in the centre,] clearly distinguishable, and of a smooth surface comparatively free from lines; under these aspects it indicates fidelity, loyalty, and an equable disposition.

Too narrow in the centre, it betrays malignity, injustice, and deceit, often accompanied by avarice. If it is much wider under the Mount of Mercury than under that of Saturn, it betrays a degeneration from generosity to avarice. Narrow under the Mount of Mercury, it denotes a more or less continual anxiety about reputation.

Too large and wide throughout its extent, it signifies imprudence, or even folly; and this is so even when there are other signs denoting prudence in the hand.

The quadrangle much filled up with little lines is a sign of a weak head.

If it is so badly traced as to be almost invisible as to its boundaries, it signifies misfortune, and a malignant, mischievous character.

It must be remembered that it is in the quadrangle that we search for the "Croix Mystique" [q.v.].

A well-coloured and well-formed star is a great indication of truth and trustworthiness. Such a subject is pliable, and can easily be dealt with by fair means, [especially by women;] such subjects generally make very considerable fortunes by their own merit.

A line from the quadrangle to the Mount of Mercury foretells the patronage and protection of the great.

## The Rascette and Restreintes

These are the names given to the wrist and bracelets of life [vide map]. According to some writers, the first or upper line only is called the rascette, the inferior ones being known as the restreintes; for my part, I prefer to name the entire region the rascette, and the lines traced across it the bracelets of life.

The bracelets of life are so called because each is said to be the indication of twenty-five to thirty years of life. I have found that in ninety-nine cases out every hundred a bracelet of life gives about twenty-five to twenty-seven years of life, and even when the line of life is short a well-braceleted rascette will still ensure a long life to the subject.

Three lines clearly and neatly traced denote health, wealth, good luck, and a tranquil life. The clearer the lines the better is the general health of the subject.

If the first line is chained we find a laborious life, but good fortune resulting therefrom.

If the lines are altogether badly formed it is a sign of extravagance.

A cross in the centre of the rascette, as at *m,* in Plate V, is a sign of a hard life, ending with good fortune and quietude.

An angle in the rascette, [as at *m,* in Plate VIII,] is a sign of inheritances and of honours in old age. To this will be added good health if a cross appear in this angle, [as at *i,* in Plate IX].

If the bracelets of life break into points converging towards the base of the line of Saturn, it is a sign of lying and vanity.

A star in the centre of the rascette will mean inheritances in a lucky hand, but unchastity in a weak sensual hand.

Moon of Jupiter will signify a very long voyage indeed; in fact, the distance of the voyages may be told from the length of the lines. If the lines converge towards the Mount of Saturn, but do not join there, it is an indication that the subject will not return from the voyage. One of them, ending on the line of life, denotes probability of death upon the voyage. If the lines are absolutely parallel throughout their course the voyages will be profitable, but dangerous.

A line from the rascette straight up to the Mount of Mercury is a prognostic of sudden and unexpected wealth.

A similar line going to the Mount of Apollo is a mark of the favour and protection of some great person.

A line from the rascette near the percussion of the hand, passing through the Mount of the Moon to join the line of the liver or health, is a sign of sorrow and adversity, especially if the line be unequal and poorly traced.

# CHAPTER FIVE

## Chance Lines

We have now arrived at a point from which having carefully discussed all the regular details of cheirosophy, it is necessary that we should turn to the consideration of certain lines which appear from time to time in the hand, and which, having special significance of their own, cannot be taken account of whilst going categorically through the indications of the principal lines, and of the various combinations of them. Their number is, of course, practically unlimited, for they form themselves according to the characters and lives of individual subjects. The student will find after a time that as the ground work of cheiromancy impresses itself upon him, he will be able at once to read the indications of any line which may be shown to him, though he may never have seen one like it before. The following instances, therefore, are not given as being in any way a complete list of the "chance lines," but are subjoined as a kind of guide for the student, to enable him to decipher these "eclectic indications" whensoever and wheresoever he may find them. The following instances are, for the most part, illustrated in Plates XII, XIII, and XIV., so that there will be no difficulty in remembering their exact positions. In these figures the principal lines are drawn, but only the chance lines are lettered and referred to.

## Disposition to Fashionable Fanaticism

A line starting from the commencement of the line of life, going to the Mount of Saturn, [as at *a a,* in Plate XII], denotes a disposition to fashionable fanaticism. If such a subject is religious *at all* it will be, that he is actuated mainly by a desire to become eminent in that particular line.

A line starting from the Mount of Mars, running under the line of heart, and turning up to the Mount of Apollo, [as at *b b,* in Plate XII], indicates a determination to attain celebrity so deeply rooted, that the subject whose hand bears this line will attain that celebrity by any means.

A line barring the whole hand from the Mount of Venus to that of Mercury denotes cleverness and intelligence, arising from an affair of the heart, or from the promptings of passion.

We have in another place discussed worry lines, which are, after all, a species of chance line; any worry line which starts from a star on the Mount of Venus denotes that some one very dearly beloved has died.

Two worry lines, extending parallel from the Mount of Venus to that of Mars, denote the pursuit of two love affairs at the same time, and a star joined to these lines denotes that the pursuit has ended in disaster.

A curved line extending from the Mount of Mercury to that of the Moon, [as at d d, Plate XII]signifies presentiments and occult powers. Such a subject, if his line of head decline upon the Mount of the Moon, will have great powers as a medium.

## Sign of Whole-Life Disturbance

If, with a chained line of heart, a line from the Mount of Venus touch it under-

# Plate XII

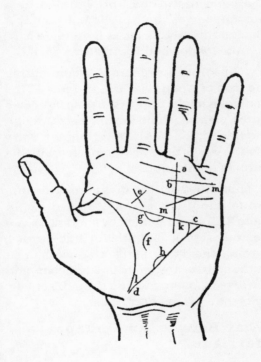

**Modifications of the Principal Lines**
**The Quadrangle and the Triangle**

neath the Mount of Mercury, [as at a a, in Plate XIII] it is a sign that the whole life has been disturbed and worried by a woman [or vice versa in a female hand]. A black point on this [as at b, in Plate XIII] signifies widowhood or widowerhood.

A line from the Mount of Venus cutting the line of Apollo, [at *c c,* in Plate XIII.,] denotes a misfortune at the time indicated by the point at which the line cuts through the line of life. If it cuts through in early life, the misfortune was connected with the parents of the subject.

Quantities of little rays across the line of life into the quadrangle, [as at e e, in Plate XII,] accompanied by short nails, are a certain sign of quantities of little worries, estrangements of friends, etc., occasioned by the spirit of argument and criticism, and the love of teasing which the subject has, by reason of his short nails.

## What Betrays an Unhappy Marriage?

A line extending from a star on the Mount of Venus to a fork under the finger of Saturn [as at d d, in Plate XIII] betrays an unhappy marriage.

A line starting from the Mount of Venus, and ending in a square in the palm of the hand, [any part,] [as at *f f,* in Plate XII,] is significant of a narrow escape from marriage with a scoundrel, or with an extending from the Mount of Venus to that of Saturn, with a similar island in the line of fortune, both at the points representing the same age, [vide Plate V] [as at a and b in Plate XIV,] indicate seduction.

A line going from a star on the Mount of Venus to the Plain of Mars, and then turning up to the Mount of Apollo, where it meets a single ray, [as at *c c,* in Plate XIV] fortells a great inheritance from the death of a near relation.

A quantity of little lines on the percussion, at the side of the Mount of Mercury, [as at d, in Plate XIV] indicate levity and inconstancy, especially if the Mounts of Venus and of the Moon are highly developed.

These few instances will, I am sure, be sufficient to explain the method of interpreting chance lines. It will be observed that they are read carefully with reference to the mounts and lines which they cross throughout their course, and according to the signs which meet and interrupt them.

The student has now traversed the entire field of Cheirosophy. It only remains for me now to give my readers a few illustrative types, before closing this manual with a few remarks on the method of proceeding in making a cheiromantic examination of a subject.

## A Few illustrative Types

I propose here to describe a few types of character and of profession; that is to say, I propose to set forth the collected signs and formations which indicate certain conditions of mind, with the probable effects of those conditions upon the subject, as regards his choice of a profession, or his walk in life.

For instance: take a hand which betrays a murderous or homicidal tendency; in this hand you will find the general complexion to be very red, or very livid; if the former, the tendency to murder arises from fury and momentary fits of anger; if the latter, the whole instinct of the subject is evil. The first phalanx of the finger of Mercury will be heavily lined, and at the

# Plate XIII

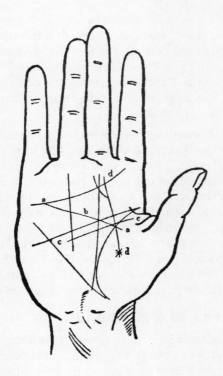

**Chance Lines**

base of the line of life will [probably] be found a sister line. the line of head will be deeply traced and thick, having probably a circle upon it, and being generally joined to the line of heart, and separate from the line of life. The nails short, the line of life thick at the commencement, and spotted with red, and the line of head twisted across the hand. All these signs collected in a hand are an infallible indication of a murderous instinct.

Take another example: in this hand we find the line of head twisted and very red, a grille is placed upon the Mount of Mercury, and the whole hand is dry and thin, having the joints developed on the fingers. From the third phalanx of the little finger, sundry small lines go on to the mount, which latter is also scarred with a deep strong ray. This is the hand of a thief, and the impulse of theft will be found to be almost [if not quite] insurmountable.

## Marks of Falsehood

Falsehood,—i.e., a general tendency to deceit —is always very clearly marked in the hand, and is marked by a number of different signs, any one of which by itself is a sufficient indication of a strong tendency in that direction. These are: a high Mount of the Moon, upon which the line of head is forked, and on which are found small red points; the thumb is short, and on the inner surfaces of the phalanges of the fingers there appears a kind of hollowing out or sinking in of the flesh. The line of head is generally separated from that of life by a space which is filled with a number of confused lines.

In conversing with a subject in whose hands you have seen all, or any, of these signs, bear in mind what we have said under the heading of Cheirology.

Another very characteristic hand is the voluptuous, or pleasure-loving hand. The fingers are smooth and pointed, having the third, or lower phalanges, swollen; the whole hand is plump and white, the palm strong, and the thumb short, giving it sensitiveness. The Mount of Venus is high. Such subjects are impressionable, and liable to fall into grave errors; they are sensual, vain, and egoists, always actuated by motives of pleasure. Women who have these hands are always dangerous, for they are subtle and unscrupulous in their pursuit of enjoyment, and often exercise a most fatal influence upon men into whose lives they come.

## Principles of Desbarrolles

Adrien Desbarrolles, in his later and larger work on the science, devotes a considerable space to the indications of various professions. It would be beyond the scope of a work like the present one to go into the matter as fully as he does at page 350 of that volume, but a short *resume* of his leading principles may not be out of place in a chapter on illustrative types.

Of an artist, the sign is of course primarily the artistic hand, but our author goes further. He discusses the various modifications which betoken different classes of painting; thus:—the flower painter will have the Mount of Venus high with long fingers, and a large thumb; [colour, detail, and perseverance; the painter of still life will have rather squared fingers and the Mount of Mercury; [exactitude and science;] the painter of battle pieces will have the Mount of Mars developed, indicating the natural taste of the subject. He points out the fact that painters with squared fingers always paint what they can actually see rather than what they merely imagine.

## Signs of Different Professions

In a doctor's hand we shall find the Mount of Mercury rayed with the line of

# Plate XIV

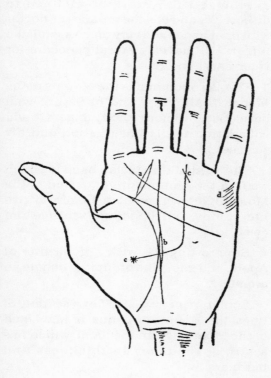

**Chance Lines**

Apollo clearly traced. The doctor whose hands bear the Mount of the Moon well developed will always be inclined to discoveries and electicism, and the doctor with hard hands and very much spatulated fingers will have a natural penchant for veterinary surgery.

The astronomer has the Mounts of the Moon, of Mercury, and of Saturn well developed, with long knotty fingers to add calculation to his imagination and his science.

The horticulturist has a hand in which we find the Mounts of Venus and of the Moon high; with spatulate fingers to give him energy, and long fingers to give him detail.

Square fingers, with a good line of Apollo and good line of Jupiter, denote an architect.

Sculpture betrays itself by a scarcity of lines, the Mounts of Venus, of Mars, and of the Moon high in the hand, which has a strong tendency to thickness and hardness.

Literary men have always the Mounts of Jupiter and of the Moon developed; the latter particularly, if the taste lies in the direction of poetry. Literature gives, as a rule, soft spatulate or square hands, with the joints [especially that of matter (the second) slightly developed. Literary critics have always short nails and high Mounts of Mercury.

Among musicians execution is the domain of subjects whose fingers are spatulate, and whose Mount of Saturn is high, whose nails are short, and whose joints are developed, with the Mount of the Moon prominent, long thumbs, the Line of Apollo, and [as a rule] the Girdle of Venus. Melody generally gives smooth fingers with mixed tips, the prevailing mount being that of Venus.

The actor has fingers which are either spatulate or square, the Mount of Venus developed, and the line of head forked. The line of heart turns up slightly towards the Mount of Mercury, and, as a rule, a line runs from the Mount of Mars to that of Apollo.

I have selected the above illustrative types from those given by M. Desbarrolles, as being those which, by repeated and careful examination, I have found to be, with extremely few exceptions, completely correct. Their explanations are easily found, and the student will, in a very short time, be able, immediately on seeing a hand, to tell the subject what is his profession.

# CHAPTER SIX

## Science of Cheirosophy

Many years ago I bought a second-hand sextant at a marine store. I was not going on a long journey, and I had absolutely no need of the sextant, but I bought it because it was a beautifully finished instrument, because there was something strange, incomprehensible, mysterious, and therefore fascinating, about it and because it was very cheap. When I had got it I did not know what to do with it; I could not use it, for I knew not how, and following the ordinary course of things, it was put away to get rusty and impracticable, without ever having been of the slightest use to me. I mention this apparently irrelevant circumstance because whenever I see a work on cheirosophy in the possession of anyone, I always think of my sextant, and wonder whether they, too, having taken up the science of cheirosophy because it is strange, apparently incomprehensibly mysterious [to them.] and therefore fascinating, have any idea of how to put their knowledge into operation, or whether, after playing inquisitively with the science for a time, they will let it lie by and become rusty and useless. It is urged by these considerations that I have decided to write this, so as not to load my readers with a quantity of knowledge, with a complicated instrument, that they cannot make use of, and derive a practical benefit from.

## How to Read Hands?

Much has been said in works on cheiromancy on the condition of the subject at the time of the examination, his mental and physical state, and so on, but think that all these things are, to a very great extent, immaterial. The only things to be borne in mind are [*selon moi*] that the hands should not be too hot or too cold, and that they should not have just been pulled out of a tight glove, and above all things, that there should be a good light. The hand should be held in an oblique position as regards the light, so as to throw the lines and formations into relief. With this object in view, also, the fingers should be slightly bent, so as to contract the palm and accentuate the lines, for it must be observed that the hands fold upon the lines, though the lines are not formed by the folding. If it is quite convenient, the morning is the best time to examine a hand, but it is practically immaterial if the cheirosophist has had any experience.

Lastly, in reading a hand, to whomsoever it belongs, you must never hesitate to take it in your own hands and hold it firmly. These short preliminaries being attended to, you will commence your examination. It is far better to examine the whole hand carefully and silently till its indications are quite clear in your own mind, and then to speak promptly and boldly, than to decipher the indications slowly one after another, reading one tentatively, with a view to ascertaining its correctness, before going on to another.

## Simplicity of the science

The great thing that I desire to impress upon the minds of my readers is the simplicity of the science. Adrien Desbarrolles, in his advanced work on the science, says: "That which prevents beginners from succeeding immediately in cheiromancy is that they find it too simple, and think it necessary to go beyond it to arrive at something more pretentious, more confused, more difficult, and more impossible to understand. They do not want an easily understood science. For many people a science which is simple, is not a science at all; they strive and strive, racking their brains in search of a truth which is at their very hands, and which they can find nowhere else."

Having taken a hand in yours, first you must examine the line of life, to see what effects health and the great events of life have had upon the condition of the subject. Next look at the phalanx of will, and see how far it is controlled or influenced by the phalanx of logic. Then you will note the tips of the fingers, seeing also whether they are smooth or whether they have the joints developed, and whether any particular phalanx or set of phalanges is or are longer or more fully developed than the others; this will tell you whether the subject is governed by intuition, by reason, or by material instinct. Then notice whether the fingers are long or short. At first you can hardly tell whether they are long or short, but after a little time you will be able to judge at once of length or shortness by comparison with the other hands you have seen; the same remarks apply to the thumb.

You have already noticed whether the hands are soft or hard, now you will turn your attention to the palm, to see what mount or mounts govern the instincts, and how those mounts are governed in turn by primary or secondary lines. Then go back to the line of life, and examine the line of fortune, noting whether the latter is broken, and if so, search on the mounts for signs to teach you the cause and interpretation of the break. Then examine carefully the lines of head and heart, and the secondary lines with the signs which may modify their indications. Be careful not to predict a future event from a sign which is evidently that of a past one: a sign which, though visible, is effaced or quasi-effaced, is that of a past event; a sign which is clear and *well coloured* is that of a present circumstance; and a sign which is only just visible, as it were, beneath the surface of the skin, is that of a future event.

Whenever you see a star, a cross, or any other sign in an apparently inexplicable position, you must search the principal lines and the mounts for an explanation. The explanation will often be found in a mark on the line of fortune or in a worry line. at the same time look at the Mount of Jupiter, for this will often, by being good, counteract the evil indications of a sign, and at the Mount of Mars to see whether the subject has that resignation which will give him calm, and even happiness, through whatever circumstances may assail his life.

When you have examined everything, strike a balance, as it were, noting what signs contradicted or counteracted by others, and what is, in fact, the whole indication of the hand. Speak boldly, and never mind offending people by what you tell them; what you tell them is *the truth,* and they need not have let you know it. I always warn people that what I shall tell them will be the actual truth, and not a string of complimentary platitudes; and I always ask people not to show me their hands if they have anything to conceal. If, after this, they still persist in having their hands read, I say boldly whatever I see there, without caring about the feelings of the subject. "Physicians are, some of them, so pleasing and conformable to the humour of the patient, as they press not the true cure of the disease; and some others are so regular in proceeding according to art for the disease, as they respect not sufficiently the condition of the patient. Take one of a middle temper, or, if it may not be found in one man, combine two of either sort; and forget not to call as well the best acquainted with your body as the best reputed of for his faculty."—Francis Bacon, "Of Regimen of Health," 1625.

## An Interesting experience

With an account [by way of illustration of the above maxims] of an interesting experience of mine now some years old, I close this chapter, and with this chapter this manual. I have had but one object in view during its composition—clearness; I can only hope that I have been successful in attaining that object, and if my introductory argument has had any power to commend this science to the consideration of unbiassed and discriminating minds, I shall feel that I have not wasted the labours of the years that are past.

A few years ago I had left my papers and goose-quills on a mangificent summer's afternoon, and had betaken myself to a garden-party in one of our prettiest suburbs. As has often been the case, my arrival was the signal for a chorus, "Here's the Cheiromant, let's get our fortunes told." In vain I remonstrated that I was out for a holiday, in vain I pleaded ill-health, ill-temper, and ill-manners; the torrent of silvery persuasion still flowed on, till at last I said :—

Listen to me; if it will amuse you, I will read *one* pair of hands for you, but they must be those of a complete stranger, and no one must ask me to repeat the experiment." Half-a-dozen pairs of hands were put forward, and from among them I chose those belonging to a childish face and a mass of sunny hair, which I had certainly never seen before. I said to her – "If you like, I'll read you hands for the amusement of all the these people, *but,* before I begin, if there is anything in your life that you have the least objection to the whole world knowing, say so at once, and I'll read someone else's."

"Oh dear no!" replied she; "My life has been utterly uneventful, go on." I looked at her hands, then at her,—still the laughing, childish face, and the calm, untroubled eyes,—and said:—

"How dare you tempt Providence like this out of pure bravado? *You know* perfectly well that there are events in your life which you don't want every one to know, and yet disbelieving [at present] in a science of which, [knowing nothing of it,] you are not in a position to give an opinion, you hold out your life's history for the amusement of a garden-party crowd. If you still insist, I will tell you your life here and now, but I should suggest that we should take a turn round the lawn, and then you will come back and tell these people that everything I have told you is absolutely correct."

She thought for a moment, and said: "There is nothing I am ashamed of; but in case you are making some horrible mistake, I'll hear my hands read in private." So we walked round the lawn.

"Well," said I, "you look about nineteen, and as if you had never had a trouble in your life, but you have had the most terrible time of it that I have ever seen written on a hand so young as yours. You have been married twice, and this, of all things, strikes me in your hand, that you married your second husband when your first husband was alive. Your first marriage was an affair of pique, an impulse of your foolish head, and was a miserable one; your second was an affair of heart, a love-match, but it was extremely bad for you from a commercial, material point of view. Even now, whilst you walk here with a smile on your lips and a racquet in your hand, you are undergoing some mental agony: let me congratulate you on being the most astounding—actress, shall I say?—that I have ever come across."

She was silent for a moment, and then said: "What I am going to tell you no one but my maid, who is in Chicago now, has ever known, and I tell it you as a reward for speaking so boldly in the face of the magnificent lie I told you just now. I am an American, and came here with some people today, and don't know a soul in the place; I am twenty-three [though I don't look it]. At eighteen I quarreled with my people, and in a fit of rage married, simply to get rid of them. My husband turned out a scoundrel and knocked me about, to speak plainly, and after a year we were divorced. When I was twenty I fell in love

160

for the first time, and married a man whom I simply worshipped. We were as happy as possible, but after a few months he was struck with a fever that gradually wasted him away, and he died two years ago, leaving me simply a pauper, for during his illness his business in Chicago left him. I came over here with some friends. What you say about my present state of mind is quite true, for I saw my first husband yesterday at the Academy, and have been in a state of terror ever since. Now, if you please, we will go back and lie to the other people about what you have been telling me."

The lady left for Yokohama a few months later, and sent me her permission to publish this incident.

# CHAPTER SEVEN

## A SHORT GRAMMAR OF PALMISTRY

### Outline

**Short Hands:** Short hands judge quickly, and do not regard detail in judgment. If with pointed fingers, imagination will aid; but the whole of things only will be regarded. Short, knotted fingers—i.e., with large joints—will have good reason, and even calculation, but will not be able to analyse.

**Long Hands:** Long hands show capacity for detail. If very large also, they will overdo it, and they generally have a greater love of finish than of ability. Long fingers show feeling and susceptibility, and when also pointed, tact. In excess, with a very narrow palm, they will show tyranny. Excessively large hands are intolerant, and when knotted are given to mania.

**Long Palm:** When the palm is much longer than the fingers, and large in proportion, the capacity for detail will be lessened, and, though the subject may have good intelligence, instinct will always encroach on reason. There will be an incapacity for very fine and delicate work, either mental or manual. The subject will, however, be easily satisfied, and not given to contention or contradiction.

**Long fingers:** when the fingers are longer than the palm, the mind will be very active, and the spirit of criticism and contradiction strong. There will be a love of argument, and the memory will be very good, especially for words, and learning by heart will be easy. Long fingers, with the knot of philosophy, will find out your faults before your virtues, and it is said good husbands and good wives are not found with these hands.

**Equal hands:** When the palm and fingers are of equal length, the balance will be perfect judgment, and instinct will go hand-in-hand, detail and the whole will be justly regarded, and confidence reposed in the subject will not be found falsified.

**Hard Hands** show energy and perseverance. If hard and pointed—activity and elegance. In excess—want of intelligence, dullness, stupidity.

**Soft hands** show laziness, natural indolence of mind or body, sometimes both. Soft and spatulate—active in mind and lazy in body. Soft and square—the reverse. Soft and pointed—indolent altogether.

N.B.—Hard and soft hands have nothing to do with the skin. That may be hardened by the occupation pursued, or softened by lack of toil. The hand should be judged by the consistency when pressed.

Supple fingers show quick action and versatility. Very thick hands show selfishness and self-esteem.

**Skin:** When the hand is soft and the skin much lined, the subject will be impressionable and upright. If hard and lined—quarrelsome. All hands covered with lines show either an agitated life or ill health. A very white hand, which does not change with heat and cold, is a sign of selfishness.

**Nails:** The nails, and the ends of the fingers, show the temper of the subject. (The lines have also to be considered, of which later on.) Short and square nails show a fighting temper; if wider than they are long—obstinacy; if square at the bottom instead of curved—passionate anger. Short nails, even with a hand otherwise benevolent, show mockery, criticism, and contradiction. Very large nails, curved at the bottom—a cool and careful head for business. Almond nails—sweet temper. If they flush pink to the outer edge, there may be occasional fits of irritation, but long, narrow nails are never malicious. Thin and little nails are a sure sign of delicate health, and fluted nails show consumption, which is also often shown by the nails being very much curved towards the top, though this is also sometimes indicative of spinal complaint.

**Smooth Hands:** (Without protruding joints)—Impressionability, intuition, inspiration, caprice, quick judgment, love of art.

**Smooth-pointed:** Religion, poetry, invention, imagination, tact, want of order. Excess:— Imprudence, exaggeration, lying, fatalism, ecstasy, posing. Altogether unpractical.

**Smooth-square:** Reason, obedience, power of organization, love of art and literature, little enthusiasm. Love of the

look of order, not the trouble. Excess:—
Tyranny, intolerance, narrow-mindedness,
love of rule to despotism. These are hard
masters.

**Smooth-spatulate:** Activity, resolution,
audacity, love of comfort, of movement, of
notoriety, of manual labour. Liking for art,
but no success. Excess:—Selfishness, want
of tact, love of fault-finding. These will
annoy themselves, and aggravate others.

**Knotted Hands:** (With large protruding
joints)—Reflection, order, science. The rule
of reason. The Knot of Philosophy: (The
top joint of the fingers)—This will show a
love of reasoning, of examining and
doubting; it is a sign of independence of
character. It is an advantage with a long
and strong thumb, with the second
phalange well formed, but with a weak
thumb it will tend to error and obstinacy,
especially if the fingers are pointed.

**Knotted-Pointed:** These hands are quick
to perceive, to observe, to understand. A
love of truth and reality, and, at the same
time, refinement and appreciation of the
beautiful. But there will be a continual fight
between inspiration and analysis, religion
and controversy, independence and piety.

166

There will be originality in art, but no success because art will be stifled by calculation.

**Second Phalange:** This should be a little longer than the first, and should be rather thick. When the first and second are of the same length and the thumb is relatively longer than the other fingers, it will show a very strong and sensible character, who will rule with reason and without tyranny. If the same thumb is of only medium length, there will be no rule over others, but passive resistance, and a strong and wise character. With the first phalange short and the second long and thick, the character will be reasonable, but liable to indecision; with clear views, the subject will make counsel over-prudence, he will balance between desire and execution, 'letting I dare not wait upon I will', and though an excellent counsellor to others, he will never profit by it himself. A good strong first phalange, with a long thick second, and the knot of philosophy will, unless the lines are very adverse, lead to success and fortune.

**Third Phalange:** (This is also called the Mount of Venus.) If very thick and long, high and encroaching on to the middle of the hand, the subject will be governed by passion; if medium and in harmony with the rest of the hand—affectionate and benevolent; if weak and flat—cold-hearted, and unless the line of heart be good, selfish. A subject who has the first long and the third much developed will govern by force of will, and love his friends and all humanity; he will be affectionate without reason, firm and constant. A subject with the second and third most developed will govern his passions by reason, but reason is feeble if will is weak, in this case the second may take the place of the first, but his life will be a continual struggle. A subject who has the first and second feeble and the third much developed, gives us but little hope of a good character; changeable and inconstant, he will be tormented by fancy and temper, be unable to keep a secret, and probably will also be melancholy.

A thumb too short shows a want of decision, but if wide and heavy at the point, it will mean obstinacy, particularly if the joint is knotty and projecting. The wider the phalange, the more pig-headed the subject; it is also a sign of bad temper, passionate anger, and want of moderation in all things.

If a hand is soft, but has the first phalange long, the subject will work from duty, not from a love of it. A spatulate hand with a short thumb is wanting in perseverance, undecided, trying everything, often loving and amiable. But if the second is well developed, uncertainty ceases, the short thumb will give quick impressions, and good judgment will ensure success.

**A long first phalange**—a man of will. A long second phalange—a man of intellect. A long third phalange—a man of heart. If the thumb bends inwards towards the fingers—avarice. If outwards—generosity, sometimes extravagance. Straight— prudence and good sense. A thumb set low down on the hand shows talent. Nearly all great men have large thumbs.

**First Finger:** (Called the finger of Jupiter)— Should be long relatively to the other fingers, and straight; this will give thought and economy. Pointed—Quick apprehension, intuition, love of reading. Square—Love of truth. Spatulate (very rare),—Error, exaggerated action; Pointed with the others square—serious thought, artistic talent (if with a good line of Apollo). First phalange relatively long—religion. Second phalange relatively long—ambition.

Third phalange relatively long—love of rule, pride. All short—want of thought, little contemplation. It is very important to artists to have a good first finger; it should be pointed.

**Second finger :** (Called the finger of Saturn)—It is not good to have this finger much longer than the others. Pointed (very rare)—Frivolity, carelessness. Square.—Prudence, grave character. Too square—sadness. Spatulate.— Activity. Too spatulate—superstition. First phalange relatively long—melancholy. Second phalange relatively long—love of agriculture. With the Knot of Philosophy—love of exact science. Third phalange relatively long—avarice.

**Third finger:** (Called the finger of Apollo)—Represents art, fame, and riches. Pointed— Artistic feeling and intuition. If with all the others in opposition—frivolity and boasting. Square—Truth and reason in art and in life. With bad lines great love of riches. Spatulate—Love of colour, of movement in art, dramatic talent. Many actors have this finger, and in artists it signifies painters of animal or genre subjects. First phalange relatively long—noble love of art. Second phalange relatively long—love of form, of display, vanity, desire to shine, love of riches.

**Fourth Finger:** (Called the finger of Mercury)—It is good that this finger should be straight and long, and if the subject is to rule other people, 'to turn them round his little finger', it should rise above the first knot of the third finger. Pointed—Eloquence, tact, diplomacy, aptitude for mystic science. Excess:— Ruse, finese, trickery. Square—Reason in science, love of the abstract, good at teaching, good at business. Spatulate—Mechanical skill, love of machinery. Excess—Theft. First phalange relatively long—love of science, eloquence, skill. Second phalange relatively long—industry, common sense, good at business, love of argument. Third phalange relatively long—scheming, evil eloquence, lying. Very long altogether—the sign of a savant.

If when the hands are held open and loose, the first and second fingers fall naturally widest, apart, it will show independence of though; if the third and fourth are widest, independence of action. If both are very wide, great originality and self-reliance. If the fingers naturally curl up towards the palm when so held, the subject will be conventional.

When the third phalanges of all the fingers are thick to the root, it is a sign of greediness, or, at least, of a love of good things to eat and drink. When the third phalanges of all the fingers incline downwards below the mounts, it shows nervousness, some-times extreme cowardice. If the first phalanges hollow and curve upwards —avarice. Reversed, when they turn back very far—extravagance. Thumb inclining inwards—avarice and selfishness. Outwards—generosity to prodigality.

(The inclination of the fingers towards each other requires much study; and none of the chiromantists I have enocountered seem to have sufficiently considered it. The few rules laid down above are those I have never known to fail but much yet remains to be discovered on this important point).

## On Reading the Hands

With regard to the difference in the lines of the right and left hands, which is one of the greatest difficulties in palmistry, I think it may be broadly stated that in the left is found what is intended for you in life, and in the right what you do with it. The left is the passive hand, the right the active. The outline of the hand, like the natural disposition, is hereditary, and it is impossible to alter it to any great degree; but the lines show the habits you encourage, the character you become, and the events that modify or establish that character, and therefore the lines of the hand are always changing, more or less according to the eventfulness, mental and physical, of the life led. It is absolutely necessary that the outline of a hand should be thoroughly understood before any attempt is made to study the lines.

When about to read the hands of your subject, you should take the left in your own, and, holding it palm downwards, look carefully at the outline. You will then be able to judge as to the class of hand to which it belongs—long or short, pointed, spatulate, or square, with or without knots, shape of the nails, etc—telling of the temper, tact, judgment, will, quickness of apprehension, and so on, of your subject. Then turn the hand over and press the palm, so as to tell of the hardness or softness of the hand, as energy or laziness is the keynote of a character, and modifies all other signs. The hand should then be laid *palm upwards* on a sheet of paper, and the tops and bottoms of the fingers and edge of the outline dotted with a pencil, so as to be sure of the measurements being correct and in exact proportion. The subject should then hold the hand in an easy position, slightly horizontally, before the student, who should carefully draw the outline. The hand should then be laid flat downwards upon a table in a good light for the drawing of the lines, which, after being first drawn in pencil, should be corrected and redrawn in ink. This done, the student should note down upon another sheet of paper the other things of the hand, the shape and height of the mounts, the colour of the lines, the feel of the hand and texture of the skin, shape of the nails, etc. the right hand should then be observed, and, if time allows, a drawing should also made of it as well, and in the same manner; but if time presses and the subject becomes impatient, it will be sufficient to note down carefully the differences between the two hands. The drawings should then be thoroughly studied by the student with the help of the grammar, note being taken of every peculiarity, no one sign being taken by itself without the corroborative evidence of the other; and against every conclusion drawn, the reasons for so thinking should be noted for future experience, and finally a careful summing-up should be given to the subject, and the drawings of the hands and the full notes written by the student should be entered into a book kept by him for the purpose.

The student should never attempt to read a hand verbally until after at least six months of careful drawing and study, as I am sure it is completely impossible to carry all the rules and directions of this difficult science at once in the memory, and to produce correct deductions spontaneously at the sight of a new and unstudied hand; though after a time, of course, it becomes possible to tell a character truly at a glance and events correctly without a moment's hesitation. But I am sure if students would have the energy and patience to follow the suggestions made above as to the drawing of hands, we should have less false conclusions arrived at, and fewer innocent people would be frightened out of their wits by the terrible and startling events prognosticated by the amateur palmist.

# GLOSSARY OF TERMS

**Finger and mount of Jupiter**—the first finger with the mount at its base.

**Finger and mount of Saturn**—the second finger with the mount at its base.

**Finger and mount of mercury**—the fourth finger with the mount at its base.

**Mount of Mars**—the first, the space between the thumb and the bottom of the Mount of Jupiter; the second, the mount on the outside of the hand, immediately below the Mount of Mercury.

**Mount of Luna**—space between the Mount of Mars and the wrist.

**Mount of Venus**—large mount at the base of the thumb.

**Line of life, or Vital**—line that encircles the Mount of Venus.

**Line of Head, or Cerebral**—line rising between the thumb and first finger, and crossing the hand horizontally.

**Line of Heart, or Mensal**—line crossing the hand horizontally beneath the Mounts.

**Line of Fate, or Saturnian**—line running perpendicularly up the from the wrist to the base of the second finger.

**Line of Fortune, or Solar**—line running perpendicularly up the hand to the base of the third finger.

**Line of Health, or Hepatica**—line running perpendicularly up the hand to the base of the fourth finger.

**Line of Intuition, or Lunar**—line running in a curve from the Mount of Luna to the base of the fourth finger.

**Ring of Venus**—line running horizontally from between the first and second fingers towards the fourth.

**Bracelets, or Rascettes**—lines encircling the wrist.

**Percussion**—side of the hand, opposite the thumb.

**Plain of Mars**—the palm of the hand.

**Quadrangle**—space between the Heart and Head Lines.

**Triangle**—space between the Lines of Head, Life, and Fate, or Health.

**Marriage Lines**—lines running horizontally across the Mount of Mercury.

www.pilgrimsbooks.com

For more details about Pilgrims and other books published
by them you may visit our website at
www.pilgrimsbooks.com
or
for Mail Order and Catalogue
contact us at

Pilgrims Book House
B. 27/98 A-8 Nawab Ganj Road
Durga Kund Varanasi 221010
Tel. 91-542-2314060
Fax. 91-542-2312456
E-mail: pilgrimsbooks@sify.com

PILGRIMS BOOK HOUSE (New Delhi)
1626, Raj Guru Road Pahar Ganj, Chuna Mandi
New Delhi 110055
Tel: 91-11-23584015, 23584019
E-mail: pilgrim@del2.vsnl.net.in
E-mail: pilgrimsinde@gmail.com

PILGRIMS BOOK HOUSE (Kathmandu)
P O Box 3872, Thamel, Kathmandu, Nepal
Tel: 977-1-4700942,
Off: 977-1-4700919,
Fax: 977-1-4700943
E-mail: pilgrims@wlink.com.np

# MORE TITLES ON
# ASTROLOGY AND PALMISTRY
# FROM PILGRIMS PUBLISHING

- **Pocket book of Palmistry** ................. Edwin A Symmes
- **Gems and their Occult Powers:**
  *An analytical description of*
  *mystical properties of precious and*
  *semi-precious stones* ................................... P N Scherman
- **Indian Astrology**
  *Ashtottari and Vinshottari Dashas* ..... Ramniklal R Mody
- **The Laws of Scientific Hand Reading**
  ........................................................ William G. Benham
- **Practical Astrology** ............. Comte C. de Saint Germain
- **Palmistry Simply Explained** ..................... James Ward
- **The Study of Palmistry** ..... Comte C. de Saint Germain